Policymaking

for School Library Media Programs

by Marian Karpisek

American Library Association
Chicago and London 1989

Marian Karpisek is supervisor of Library Media Services for the Salt Lake City School District, and an adjunct professor in the School of Library and Information Science at Brigham Young University.

Cover designed by Michael Brierton
Text designed by Charles Bozett

Composed by ALA Books on a BestInfo Wave4 pre-press system and output by Master Typographers on a Linotronic L500

Printed on 50-pound Glatfelter B-31, a pH-neutral stock, and bound in 10-point Carolina cover stock by Versa Press, Inc.

The paper used in this publication meets the minimum requirements of American National Standard for Information Sciences—Permanence of Paper for Printed Library Materials, ANSI Z39.48-1984. ∞

Library of Congress Cataloging-in-Publication Data

Karpisek, Marian E.

    Policymaking for school library media programs / by Marian Karpisek.
       p. cm.
       Bibliography: p.
       Includes index.
       ISBN 0-8389-0520-X (alk. paper)
       1. School libraries—Administration—Decision making. 2. Media programs (Education)—Management—Decision making. I. Title.
    Z675.S3K25 1989
    025.1′978223—dc20   89-15109

Printed in the United States of America.
93 92 91 90 89   5 4 3 2 1

To my parents, Ruth and Sam Ream

Contents

Illustrations

Preface

The school library media program is an essential element of the educational program in a school. In an age where information is increasing at an ever-expanding rate, the library media program provides the link between the limited resources of the classroom and the unlimited resources of the larger community. The recent focus on critical thinking skills and student-centered learning emphasizes the importance of the library media program in the educational setting.

The school library media *center* is the *place* within the school setting having a diverse collection of materials and resources. It is a physical facility containing books, furniture, audiovisual materials, and equipment. In and of itself, the library media center is a classroom designated as an organized repository of information.

The school library media *program* is the *means* by which the resources of the center change from inert objects into active learning components that stimulate the mind and intellect of the user. The program includes the teaching of library media skills, literature appreciation, information provision, and instructional consultation. Program is the active voice of library media service.

The library media program exists within the context of the educational program of the school and district. The principal, who is the building level administrator, is responsible for all programs within the school and, as such, must be actively involved in the definition of the library media program. A close link between library media philosophy and the philosophy of the school enables the library media program to interface effectively with the educational program.

The catalyst for the library media program is the library media specialist. A library media center can exist without a library media specialist; but a library media program cannot. The specialist develops the program in order to reach each student and teacher and expand the horizons of those whom it influences.

In order to create a functional library media program, the specialist needs a clear concept of library media philosophy and the policies which support the program. POLICYMAKING FOR SCHOOL LIBRARY MEDIA PROGRAMS is intended to help practicing library media specialists develop the foundations of philosophy and policy upon which to build exciting, relevant, and resourceful programs for the school community. It provides the means for establishing program parameters and ascertaining that the library media center is not merely a designated space, but the site of an active library media program.

POLICYMAKING FOR SCHOOL LIBRARY MEDIA PROGRAMS extends beyond the definition of philosophy and policy. It provides a framework of management procedures by which the library media specialist enacts policy into practice. For example, selection policy defines guidelines for choosing materials and the accompanying procedures delineate how the acquisition process occurs.

This book is intended to help the fledgling specialist manage the administrative activities of the library media program. Options are offered, where possible, to address variations that occur from school to school. The specialist must define and construct a program that meets both the needs of the school setting and existing district confines. It is hoped that, through reading and implementing the concepts outlined in this book, the new specialist will feel confident to embark on the exciting career of a library media professional.

Acknowledgments

I wish to thank the many library media specialists who contributed to my understanding and knowledge of library media management. Salt Lake City School District Library Teacher Leaders Jean Burks, Carol Buckmiller, Darol Denison, Linda Gentry, Lori Komlos, Lynn Komlos, Theresa Magelby, Katherine Olsen, and Herb Urry were especially helpful in sharing their visions of library media service. In addition, each library media specialist in the Salt Lake City School District has provided a wealth of source material. Rob Wakefield graciously and unstintingly shared his expertise in public relations and my colleagues on the John Cotton Dana Committee reinforced these concepts. Supervisors Beverly Bagan, Connie Champlin, Betty Keefe, Retta Patrick, and Joie Taylor, among others, expanded my understanding of library media programs nationally.

A special thanks to Donna Delchambre and Ken Neal who got me started in this exciting field and to my colleague Sharyl Smith with whom I exchange ideas and challenges. Sheila Stephens and Karen Berner provided invaluable feedback by spending many hours reading and discussing the drafts of this book. Herb Bloom kept me focused on the crucial elements of the text and Ruth F. Ebbinghaus suggested substantive revisions in editing the final version. Their insight was extremely beneficial. The students in my classes at Brigham Young University served as a sounding board as I developed and refined policies and procedures.

Deep appreciation is expressed to Superintendent John W. Bennion, Assistant Superintendents Jack Keegan and Mary Jean Johnson, and the Salt Lake City Board of Education for their enthusiastic support of library media programs. Their strong commitment has been the impetus for the district's excellent programs, which have provided the basis for much of the material in this book.

Without the word processing skills of Mary H. Kowalczyk, this book could not have been completed on time. Her flawless pages made correcting drafts a joy.

My daughters, Jenny and Kris, were especially considerate and helpful while I was involved in the writing process.

Finally, this book could not have been written without the encouragement, support, and help of my husband, Bob.

CHAPTER 1

Development of the Library Media Center

The library media center is the heart of the school. The library has evolved from a simple book depository to a multifaceted media center with the potential for influencing curriculum and stimulating educational innovation and reform.

The ideal library media center is sufficiently staffed to offer a variety of services, including providing access to information, teaching library media skills, developing curriculum with teachers, and producing original materials. The philosophy of library media center management is based on the premise that the staff teams with teachers to integrate media into all areas of the curriculum, to teach the skills necessary for locating and synthesizing information, and to develop an appreciation of literature. The ideal center has abundant resources upon which to draw, including audiovisual materials and computer software as well as books. The center thus fosters the concept of education as a learning process dependent on a variety of media and resources.

This ideal center does exist in many schools. Unfortunately not all school systems are cognizant of the value inherent in an optimal library media program and, in reality, centers across the country have extremely diverse emphases. Much of this diversity can be traced to historical influences and trends. Three factors have made a substantial impact on the development of library media centers: a changing educational philosophy, emerging library media theory, and fluctuating financial support.

This chapter examines the historical background of school library media centers and the environment of district and school support. The elements of library media services are also discussed.

History

The library media center is a fairly recent arrival on the education scene. Prior to the 1960s, the concept of expanding library resources to include nonbook media was not widespread.

Since the Babylonians and Assyrians first recorded information on clay tablets, libraries have served as repositories of knowledge. Papyrus and parchment libraries extended accessibility to information. The Chinese invention of paper about A.D. 100 and the advent of the printing press in 1440 enabled the written word to be disseminated to a wider, more literate population, primarily through private libraries. Colonial settlers in America brought books with them and, as universities were built, endowed them with libraries.

The first school libraries in the United States were found in secondary schools and were often stocked with donated books. A teacher or principal supervised the circulation of these books as time permitted. The library was housed wherever there was room: in an extra classroom, a spare bookcase, or an empty closet. Initially, the library was considered to be a repository of books solely for supplementing the literature curriculum.

In 1920, the American Library Association (ALA) adopted the first standards for school libraries. These standards specified that a school library should meet the reading interests of the students in the school. They further stated that the library "must be conceived of in terms of service, in terms of housing, of equipment, and of appropriately selected books, magazines, and visual materials of all kinds which relate to the working and recreational needs of pupils and teachers. It must be conceived of in terms of intelligent, skillful, sympathetic librarianship."[1]

Before these Certain Standards, so-called for the chair of the committee, C. C. Certain, school libraries had no universal standards. The Certain Standards, established nationally recognized guidelines for school libraries. For the first time, school librarians in the 1920s and 1930s had a point of reference upon which to build philosophy, establish goals, and implement practices.

Although the Certain Standards must be applauded for being the first set of standards, they were fairly limited in their impact. Library service was not seen as a component of the school's curriculum, but as a separate entity with the primary purpose of supplying appropriate materials to meet the student's reading interests. The curriculum outside of the literature program was, by and large, ignored. This concept of the library as an adjunct facility was so ingrained that decades passed before the concept of systematic integration into the curriculum evolved.

The 1920 standards were instrumental in awakening educational decision makers to the need for including libraries in the secondary school accreditation process. When the standards for accreditation required secondary schools to have libraries and specified evaluation criteria, districts took action. Although some districts established libraries only to meet accreditation requirements, the perception of the school library as an essential aspect of secondary education was strengthened.

Unfortunately, elementary schools were not required to be accredited and, as a result, there was no simultaneous movement to establish elementary school libraries. Some visionary school districts, however, recognized the advantages of library service at all levels. For these isolated elementary librarians, the 1920 standards provided substance and direction for their efforts.

The American Library Association revised the standards in 1945 in *School Libraries for Today and Tomorrow*. These standards broadened the philosophy of the 1920 standards by defining the library "as an active service agency integrated with the learning program of the school, not as an adjunct to it." Students were encouraged to become discriminating users of print and audiovisual materials. School librarians were urged to provide materials and services to assist in the growth and development of the individual and to help students acquire desirable social attitudes and cultural growth.[2] Unfortunately, the standards gave no directions for implementation of these lofty goals.

The 1945 standards expanded the concept of library services from simple reading enrichment to active curriculum involvement. Teacher/librarian planning was a new idea that involved the librarian peripherally with curriculum. Nevertheless, the emphasis was on supplying necessary print and audiovisual materials rather than on working with students and teachers to utilize the materials. Instruction continued to be directed at large groups rather than individuals.

Large scale federal aid to school libraries began with the National Defense Education Act (NDEA) in 1958. School libraries were the beneficiaries in the race to upgrade the American educational system after the Soviet Union stunned the world by launching *Sputnik*. American education was deemed to be sadly lacking in science, math, and foreign languages. These subjects became the first to be targeted for NDEA grants. Later grants allowed expenditures for materials in other curriculum areas and for media training for librarians and teachers.

How districts, schools, and teachers utilized these federal funds was an indication of how seriously they accepted the concept of media as a viable vehicle for conveying curriculum content. Some districts refused to participate in the program and did not receive the benefits. Other districts participated by providing matching funds without a plan for utilization. In these districts, expensive equipment was relegated to dusty corners and materials sat untouched on library shelves.

Those districts that benefited most from NDEA funds were those that developed a philosophy for incorporating the new technology and materials into the curriculum. These districts recognized that central administration of materials and equipment within the school would be most beneficial. Appointment of an audiovisual specialist to facilitate use was a popular solution. In other schools, librarians expanded their field of expertise and took on the added responsibilities. Changing the role or adding personnel, however, was not the sole ingredient to successful NDEA implementation. Schools that actively sought to broaden their curriculum with a philosophy incorporating audiovisual materials and individualized instruction were those that found success. Where this philosophy was coupled with an active library media specialist, programs flourished with the incentive funds. For the fledgling media specialists striving to develop strong programs, the 1960 standards were a beacon that guided them as they entered new waters.

The American Library Association's 1960 guidelines, *Standards for School Library Programs,* were written in response to requests from school librarians across the country who felt that there was a need for higher quantitative and qualitative standards if the concept of the school library was to grow.

The infusion of federal funds had given many librarians a vision of the impact that school libraries could make given adequate resources. Although some schools saw increased standards only as justification for indiscriminate acquisitions, professional librarians administering the programs saw a genuine need for higher standards. They could see the positive effect on achievement that occurred when students were provided with a variety of materials that met differing learning styles.

The 1960 standards made a giant leap forward as they enlarged the scope of collections and professional staff. The parameters of program, collection, and facility were expanded. It was also recommended that the librarian have teacher training as a minimum standard and, preferably, teaching experience.[3] The librarian was seen as an active participant in helping teachers prepare original materials as well as a resource person who could locate and provide materials. The 1960 standards set the stage for more fully integrating library materials into the curriculum, but retained the traditional concept of the library as an adjunct facility. The usefulness of the library in integrating material into ongoing instruction was noticed but remained underdeveloped.

The 1960 standards helped create a surge of interest in school libraries. In 1963, the Knapp School Libraries Project, sponsored by the Knapp Foundation, granted $1,130,000 to the American Association of School Librarians (AASL) for a five-year project to establish model school libraries to demonstrate the effect of quality library services at both elementary and secondary levels. At the time the grant was given, two-thirds of the elementary schools in the United States lacked a school library.[4]

The goal of the Knapp Project was to correlate schools of high quality with schools having a library program that met the 1960 standards. The five elementary and three secondary schools selected for the project were located from Long Island, New York, to Portland, Oregon.

The project had four primary objectives:

1. To demonstrate the educational value of school library programs, services, and resources when they met the national standards.
2. To promote improved understanding and use of library resources by teachers and administrators through teacher education programs in nearby colleges.
3. To guide and encourage educators and citizens to develop their own school programs.
4. To increase interest and support for school library development among educators and citizens through dissemination of information regarding the programs and their evaluation effectiveness.[5]

Various states and provinces of Canada followed the example of Knapp Project schools and established their own model school libraries to serve as local exemplary projects. The schools involved in the Knapp Project and their spin-offs were publicly recognized for creating ideal facilities and for demonstrating that the programs had a positive effect on student learning. A study evaluating the Knapp Project found that fourth- and sixth-grade students with access to a central library performed significantly higher in library-related skills such as note-taking, outlining, and expressing ideas than did a control group that did not have the same library facilities and programs.[6]

The success of the Knapp Project and educator response to NDEA funding set the stage for increased interest in school libraries. Congressional passage of Title II of the Elementary and Secondary Education Act (ESEA) in 1965 provided another leap forward for school libraries: $234,000,000 was appropriated for library and instructional materials in 1966 with an additional $80,000,000 budgeted in 1967.[7]

Eligibility specifications for ESEA Title II monies required schools to have a library. As a result, 24,000 schools [8] that had previously ignored the data supporting the value of quality libraries suddenly saw the importance of such a facility when it held the key to substantial revenues. The depth of actual commitment remained in question.

The attitude of schools and districts toward library programs was clearly evidenced by the way ESEA Title II funding was implemented. Schools and districts that were supportive of libraries financed adequate staff, facilities, and budgets. Those that did not value the services provided only the minimum needed to qualify for funding. Because schools were not required to hire professional librarians in order to comply with eligibility guidelines, 48,000 schools still had no qualified school librarians.[9] Untrained aides, parent volunteers, or teachers who wanted to escape the stresses of the classroom were pressed into providing minimal service. The idea of librarians as partners in instruction could not easily take hold under these circumstances.

It can be seen that ESEA Title II funding was sometimes a help, and sometimes a hindrance, to school library programs. Where philosophy was supportive, school libraries received a substantial qualitative boost in acquisitions. With innovative and creative librarians guiding these programs, great strides were made in moving libraries into the mainstream of curriculum.

Where philosophy merely gave token support to school libraries, ESEA Title II did little more than place volumes on shelves. These schools used the funding for items that were not selected according to student and teacher needs and were, therefore, seldom used. Indeed many schools did not know how to incorporate into their educational program the plethora of materials that suddenly appeared. Educators who administered these schools could see very little relevance in having a school library and did little, if anything, to push for continued or expanded funding. Two decades later this attitude still prevails in some districts and states.

During the late sixties and early seventies when government subsidies to school libraries were unprecedented, the educational philosophy of individualized instruction came to the forefront. As support for a teaching method using differing materials increased, enlightened schools and districts began to appreciate that libraries were the appropriate site for the integration of individualized materials. The center was seen as the place where students could work successfully with self-paced audiovisual instructional materials. More broadly, the librarian could become the resource person most able to guide the integration of materials and curriculum.

The 1969 *Standards for School Media Programs,* written jointly by members of the American Association of School Librarians and the Department of Audiovisual Instruction of the National Education Association, provided terminology and support for unified programs. The separate identities of audiovisual coordinator and librarian were merged into a single title— media specialist. The media specialist was to be an activist who would promote effective access to information. The specialist, however, remained a resource person providing materials rather than a facilitator serving as an active member of the teaching team and working with content. The 1969 standards centered on people and programs rather than on materials and their arrangement. The focus was on effective access to materials rather than on procedures of acquisition.[10] The media specialist was required to be knowledgeable in print and nonprint materials, equipment, production, and curriculum. Many states revised their certification standards to demand competency in all of these areas.

The auspicious climate in which both resources and educational philosophy fostered the development of library media centers continued until 1974 when ESEA Title II was superseded by ESEA Title IVB. The new federal category included funding for library media materials (ESEA II), for equipment (NDEA III), and for guidance, counseling, and testing materials (ESEA III). Local educational agencies were given complete control over how the grants were to be spent.[11] The dispersion of funds severely reduced the dollars available for library media materials. Although guidance, counseling, and testing were eventually removed from Title IVB in 1978, funding for library media materials never regained its previous impetus.

The decline in federal funds designated for media centers coincided with an increase in inflation, a decrease in revenue from property taxes, a decrease in student enrollments, and the closing of schools in many urban districts. None of this was beneficial to school library media centers. By the late 1970s and early 1980s, many school districts were pulling back in their commitment to library media centers. The first to retreat were districts whose philosophy and purpose had been weak in support of school library media centers and programs. Their commitment was superficial and had depended on grant-related requirements. These districts were unwilling to continue their support independently. Some districts had been committed half-heartedly; the combined pressures gave them a ready excuse to reconsider their positions. These were districts that backed good programs when the economy was supportive, but turned away from " nonessential" programs when the economy took a downswing.

There were many schools and districts, however, that lived up to their commitment. When federal and local revenues declined, they did not automatically delete library media programs. Instead, they worked to save what they felt was the backbone of the learning process. Funding was reduced only as a last resort and never to the point where programs became ineffectual. A few districts (and states) recognized that a school's academic program and the library media program that sustained it required strong support and funding to keep them both alive and growing.

Media Programs: District and School, published in 1975 by the American Association of School Librarians and the Association for Educational Communications and Technology (AECT), was partially a response to the specter of declining support. The intent of these standards was "to sustain and improve school media services at every level of operation." For the first time, library media standards acknowledged the necessity for strong district-level support services and gave recognition to their impact on school library media programs. The concept of networking was also a key addition. The standards defined service as having four aspects: instruction, design, consultation, and administration.[12]

The 1975 standards sanctioned a broadened arena of performance, but did not adequately address the necessity of involvement in the curriculum. The implications of an integrated program were considered, for example, scheduling, staff, resources, and so forth, but a strong case was not made for implementation.

The greatest lack in the 1975 standards was the dearth of qualitative descriptors. While the 1920 and 1945 standards delved into aspects of program utilization, the 1975 standards tended to emphasize quantitative requirements for program development. Quantitative standards were disheartening for the specialist working under adverse conditions, and the standards too often represented an out-of-reach goal.

ESEA Title IVB held fairly constant from 1978 to 1982 when categorical aid at the federal level ended. The Education Consolidation and Improvement Act (ECIA) of 1981, Chapter 2, also referred to as the Block Grant, replaced thirty-three categorical programs.

As in Title II of the 1974 ESEA, individual districts were given the responsibility of deciding how the Chapter 2 allocations were to be spent. Preliminary research by the American Association of School Administrators indicates that 83.5 percent of the districts surveyed used at least part of their funding to purchase computers and computer software while 80.8 percent used some part of the funds for books, instructional materials, and audiovisual equipment.[13] Whether these purchases were intended for use in library media centers or in classrooms is not clear and no comparison was made of current Chapter 2 funding for library media centers in relationship to previous categorical grants. Another recent survey revealed that of thirty-four states confirming their receipt of Chapter 2 funds, only seventeen of them "could identify the library resource projects [being] developed" with the money.[14] Further study will be required to fully assess the impact of ECIA Chapter 2.

Support for school library media programs has reverted almost entirely to local school districts because of the Block Grant concept. Shortly after the demise of categorical aid, *A Nation at Risk,* the report of the National Commission on Excellence in Education, stimulated interest in reform and accountability in education. However, the document failed to recognize the effect that school library media centers can have on improving student achievement. Both ALA and AASL responded to the omission by releasing documents supportive of library media programs. Unfortunately, these responses did not receive the widespread publicity of *A Nation at Risk*. Since that initial report, other studies have recommended improvements for education, but school library media service remains a neglected aspect and one which the library media profession needs to address more aggressively.

Nevertheless, nationwide concern for excellence in education is providing a springboard for a revitalization of quality library media programs. Budgets for library media programs are slowly but steadily increasing and may indicate an upswing in support of library media center funding.

The 1988 standards, *Information Power: Guidelines for School Library Media Programs,* are an outgrowth of a changing society and an expanding awareness of educational accountability. Four years of intense work went into the writing of these standards and widespread input from practitioners was solicited.

Recognition that the success or failure of the library media program is dependent on the library media specialist is the focus for the 1988 standards. Rather than concentrate on quantitative measures of achievement, a narrative format is used to delineate quality of service. (Quantitative material relates numerical data of schools regarded as having high levels of services.) The 1988 standards represent a quantum change from previous standards and are hailed by many library media specialists as an important step toward strengthening programs while respecting diversity.

The modification of the term *media center* to *library media center* is enhancing communication between library media specialists and their communities. Terminology does not determine service, but the public seems more supportive of the "library" concept, and it is the public that ultimately holds the purse strings.

There are exciting opportunities for library media programs in the future. To realize them, though, library media specialists must implement the new standards, and public support for excellence in education must continue. Reversing the decline in Chapter 2 funds will also be necessary. In FY89, $491 million was appropriated instead of the $580 million authorized, a decrease from the FY88 appropriation of $504 million. A temporary reprieve can be seen in PL100-297, an omnibus education bill that focuses on five areas. School library media centers stand to profit as one of those areas, as well as from inclusion in targeted assistance programs. PL100-297 block grant authorizations are $610 million for FY90, $640 million for FY91, $672 million for FY92, and $706 million for FY93.[16] It remains to be seen whether the appropriations will equal the authorization.

Effect of District Philosophy and School Policies

District Philosophy

School districts in the United States can be found at all intervals on the continuum of library media service. There are districts that provide no services at all and districts with totally integrated programs. Most districts fall somewhere in the middle. How does one determine the value placed by a district on school library media service? The following indicators can be used to assess district commitment to library media programs.

Written district philosophy. A district's educational philosophy can be read carefully to ascertain what the board of education envisions as the ultimate goals of education. A straightforward statement of support for library media programs is preferred, of course. Lacking this, philosophical expression of ideas central to library media practice can indicate a supportive climate. These ideas conceive of education as a lifelong process of learning that requires the use and synthesis of library media. The district that promotes these ideas is philosophically in tune with the library media concept. Other district philosophic statements supportive of quality library media service include those that espouse belief in the ability of every student to learn, that foster individualized instructional programs, and that recognize differences in learning styles.

School library media funding. The district's emphasis on funding is the tangible expression of its philosophy of library media service. Without adequate budgets to ensure purchase of essential materials and equipment, service is necessarily curtailed. Budgets for print materials should include sufficient monies for books, periodicals, and ephemeral items. Funding for nonprint materials should be adequate for the purchase of filmstrips, pictures, kits, computer programs, and so forth.

Audiovisual materials are effective only if they can be utilized easily and with clarity and fidelity. The equipment should not damage the materials. Old equipment, in constant need of repair and subject to unpredictable failure, does not encourage teachers to use media. Equipment should, of course, flexibly meet the needs of both large groups and individuals, and also should promote the concept of the library media center. The center, for example, is the ideal and pivotal organization to entrust with the use of microcomputers in the curriculum.[17]

Information available on databases mandates access by students. The computer explosion has districts scrambling for funds to provide sufficient hardware and software for classroom and management functions. Technology in the near future may mean equipping schools for interactive video applications with satellite dishes and cable television. Other technological advancements most certainly will require additional funding. Library media centers are establishing their own role in the acquisition and utilization of microcomputers within schools.[18] How schools respond to the possibilities and needs of new technologies is indicative of their commitment to the future of library media service.

Block Grant funds. The distribution of Block Grant funds may be an additional indicator of how much importance a district places on the library media program. A significant percentage of the allocation slated for library media programs may testify to commitment. However, Block Grant funds should not be used to supplant district financial support. Block Grant funding should be supplemental rather than basic. When Block Grant funds are spread over a variety of programs rather than targeted for library media needs, district support may be weak or nonsubstantive.

School library media center staffing. Staffing patterns in school library media centers are another indicator of district commitment to library media services. Schools staffed with a sufficient number of professionals, paraprofessionals, and aides are reflective of a district committed to effective library media service. A district supportive of the library media center would have about one professional for every 250 students, though this ratio would, of course, vary with the types of services the center provides.[19] Some districts cannot fund staffing at ideal levels, but a single professional specialist in each school is the minimum level indicative of district support of library media services. At this level, the district can be considered supportive even if revenues are inadequate to fund all programs satisfactorily and the library media program is not the only program not fully funded.

Library media center facilities. The physical design of the school library media center may be indicative of the support given by the district. This is particularly true in newer school buildings. The location, size, and furnishings of the center may all provide valuable clues to the district's philosophy. The library media center should be centrally located within easy reach of all classrooms. In older schools, built when library media centers were not part of the design, centrality to all rooms may not be possible. However, even in older schools, the space provided testifies to the importance placed on the library media center. The size of the center determines how many students can be served simultaneously. A very small facility limits student access to materials while a spacious center offers extensive possibilities for use. Furnishings indicate whether students are encouraged to browse and work independently or whether use is regimented. Comfortable chairs, carrels, and attractive nooks indicate independent use; formal table and chair arrangements reflect traditional class use.

District support staff. Districts that are supportive of school library media programs provide central office supervisory and administrative staff. District coordination and facilitation of library media programs provides focus and direction for school-level specialists.

The Montgomery County, Maryland, Public Schools, in their model library media program, have identified seven areas of district service necessary to provide articulation between schools and districts.

1. Field Services—Responsible for serving as a liaison between the central office facility and school facilities and provides guidance in local program development.
2. Selection—Responsible for organizing selection procedures, obtaining preview materials, and preparing recommended materials and equipment lists.
3. Inventory Management—Responsible for maintaining a centralized inventory of school-owned materials.
4. Cataloging and Processing—Responsible for preparing all purchased materials for circulation.
5. Distribution—Responsible for materials circulating from the central Instructional Media Center to the schools.
6. Graphics Production—Responsible for producing original instructional materials and assisting teachers in producing their own original materials.
7. Curriculum and Professional Library—Responsible for obtaining and supplying educators with the texts, professional books, and related print materials required to meet their educational needs.[20]

Districts not providing this expertise fail to integrate the library media program on a districtwide basis. Each school must go in its own direction and provide all services independently. Some services, for example, 16mm film collections, are not practical at the local school level and are usually nonexistent or minimal without a centralized facility. Other services, such as previewing of materials, purchasing, cataloging, and processing of materials, can be provided at the local school site, but are more efficient and cost effective when handled on a centralized basis.

School Philosophy

Just as each district has a philosophy regarding library media programs, so do individual schools. District philosophy affects library media programs at the organizational level while school philosophy affects the operational or implementation level. There are four key indicators of school support for effective library media programs: written philosophy, scheduling, attitudes, and collection.

Written philosophy. The existence of a written philosophy that includes a statement of commitment to the library media program is evidence of a supportive school climate. When the statement establishes library media service as a component of the curriculum, it sets the parameters for definitive objectives to be achieved.

The absence of a written philosophy containing reference to the library media center may be reflective of the weakness prevailing in the district philosophy. It may be that the school's philosophy has not been updated in many years or it may mean that the program is regarded as a supplemental, rather than an integral, part of the curriculum. When the written school philosophy does not make clear reference to the library media center, other indicators must be investigated to reveal the commitment level.

Scheduling. The schedule for utilizing the library media center can reveal how teachers conceptualize the center and its services. If an elementary school center is rigidly scheduled with classes, the center probably is seen as a separate facility where students go regularly, but one which has little relevance to the ongoing curriculum. At the secondary school level, if the center is rarely used, it is indicative of a library media program that exists outside the mainstream of the total educational program. If the schedule indicates that there are opportunities for individual student research and independent work and that classes are scheduled as needed for development of related skills, the center is probably an integral part of the school's program.

Educational staff attitudes. The attitudes toward the educational process that are exhibited by the principal(s) and teachers in a school may be reflective of attitudes toward the library media center. A staff that is enthusiastic, involved, and receptive to new ideas will be more in tune with a progressive library media program than will a traditionally minded faculty that relies exclusively on textbooks. Teachers of the former type are probably the most crucial factor in getting students to use the library media center.[21] Attitudes, though initially nonsupportive, can be changed by a specialist who communicates the goals of the center and who helps teachers see the benefits that an integrated library media program can have for students.

Collection. The materials contained in the library media center's collection can be examined and will give an indication of school commitment. The number of items on the shelves cannot be the sole criteria for judging a collection, however. More important than quantity are sufficient up-to-date materials that relate to all course offerings in the curriculum. If the materials are circulated regularly, the probability exists that the center is indeed an integral part of the school.

The four indicators, whether written or tacit, can provide a fairly accurate picture of the school's support of the library media program. They are also the key areas in which the library media specialist can provide leadership. No single factor can stand alone; however, when viewed together, these indicators provide an indication of the amount of support for library media programs.

Elements of Library Media Service

The new library media specialist enters a center with district and school parameters defined. History, educational philosophy, library media theory, and district and school philosophy have set the stage for the school-level program. Staffing, facility design, and budgets are considerations that determine, to a great extent, the amount of service that can be given. It is within the constraints of these given resources that the library media specialist works to provide effective services to students and faculty.

The library media specialist should be trained both as an educator and as a library media specialist in order to work effectively in the school library media setting. It is important that the specialist have a teaching background in order to understand the goals and curriculum of the educational institution. Additional work in the library media field is essential for handling the specialized aspects of library media service. It is not enough to be a good teacher or a good librarian; a successful specialist must be well versed in both areas. *Information Power* delineates the bridge linking the curricular aspects of teaching with those of the library media program.

To help specialists gain a perspective on library media services, David Loertscher has identified a taxonomy of library media services that covers a continuum ranging from no library media involvement in the educational program to full participation by the library media specialist in curriculum development. The eleven levels identified by Loertscher are as follows:

> *Level One: No involvement.* Teachers do not use the services or materials of the library media center.
> *Level Two: Self-Help Warehouse.* The facilities and materials are available for those who independently search for them.
> *Level Three: Individual Reference Assistance.* Individuals receive information and materials for specific needs at their request.
> *Level Four: Spontaneous Interaction and Gathering.* Individuals receive information and materials as the need arises rather than as planned.
> *Level Five: Cursory Planning.* The specialist is a problem solver who generates solutions and provides ideas, usually in an informal setting and in a brief manner.
> *Level Six: Planned Gathering.* The teacher and specialist plan in advance and materials are gathered to assist in a specific unit.
> *Level Seven: Evangelistic Outreach.* The specialist promotes multimedia individualized instruction through in-service and public relations.
> *Level Eight: Scheduled Planning in the Support Role.* The specialist formally plans to work with students in gathering, interpreting, and creating materials.
> *Level Nine: Instructional Design, Level I.* The specialist participates in each step of development, execution, and evaluation of a unit as an equal, but detached, partner with the teacher.
> *Level Ten: Instructional Design, Level II.* The library media staff participates fully in all phases of a unit, including grading and responsibility for achievement.
> *Level Eleven: Curriculum Development.* The specialist contributes to the planning and structure of the curriculum to be taught in the school or district.[22]

A look at individual schools reveals library media services occurring at all levels on Loertscher's taxonomy. This great disparity in practice is partially a matter of economics. A fully integrated library media program having significant impact on the curriculum is more costly than one that merely provides materials. The more the center is involved with curriculum design and implementation, the more extensive the staff and resources will need to be.

The number of specialists and paraprofessionals will determine, to a great extent, the level of service that is offered. To function fully at levels nine and ten on Loertscher's taxonomy, professional and paraprofessional staffing must be commensurate with the high levels described in the 1988 standards, *Information Power*. Levels seven and eight of the taxonomy require staffing at least at the level of one professional per 250 students. Even with less than the average staffing cited for high schools, the five highest levels of services should remain of paramount concern and should be offered to the greatest extent possible. In practice, this may mean that only a limited number of units can be implemented as full partnerships between teacher and specialist, but full utilization should remain a goal. Service at level eleven can occur with less than recommended staffing as this function is often performed by district-level staff or by school-level personnel during summer vacation.

Wherever a specialist is available, service at levels two through six should be adequately provided. However, if the professional is not on-site on a full-time basis, this service must be circumscribed by time constraints.

Service at level one should exist only when there is no specialist in the school. When no service is offered, one wonders whether the center is at all functional. It is hoped that the number of schools receiving no service will decline as teachers and administrators recognize the great value to the curriculum when certified library media specialists are part of the instructional team.

The taxonomy is not a ladder on which the specialist disregards lower levels once the next level is reached. Rather, with the exception of level one, it is a broad repertoire of services that should all be available. The self-help warehouse is the appropriate utilization for student browsing and for teachers looking for ideas without a specific unit in mind. The individual who requests reference assistance must receive help at the time of need, not just during a unit cooperatively planned by teacher and specialist.

It is not mandated that each level must be systematically achieved before proceeding to the next level. Level seven is not totally dependent on achievement of level six. The taxonomy, therefore, should be used as a point of reference. In the optimal setting, levels two through eleven will be operating simultaneously, each functioning appropriately according to curriculum, student, teacher, school, and district needs. It is at the higher levels of Loertscher's taxonomy, however, that optimal educational outcomes occur.

The 1988 standards, *Information Power: Guidelines for School Library Media Programs,* surpass the expectations of Loertscher's taxonomy as they recognize that an effective school library media program depends on the collaborative efforts of all who are responsible for student learning.[23] Further, the standards describe three primary functions of the library media specialist: instructional consultation, instruction, and information provision. These functions must all be present if the library media center is to be effective.

Instructional Consultation

Providing materials and resources to enhance the curriculum is a vital component of library media service. Instructional consultation demands that the specialist have good interpersonal skills, extensive knowledge of the collection, familiarity with child growth and development patterns, and a close acquaintance with the total curriculum of the school.

On Loertscher's taxonomy, instructional consultation is an aspect of service occurring at levels three through eleven. The complexity of many subjects and the varied learning styles of students require a broad approach to traditional teaching methods. The teacher who combines text with the appropriate film, videotape, or computer disk helps students enrich and expand their comprehension of the subject matter. Research has shown that varied media are not just supplemental niceties but basic aspects of good teaching. The library media specialist can help teachers match materials to the curriculum.

It is not sufficient, however, to consider instructional consultation solely as matching materials with the curriculum and working with students in the library media center. Instructional consultation encompasses several other aspects. The specialist consults with district, regional, and state agencies to keep abreast of library media information. Consultation with teachers may range from simple assistance with equipment (both before use and when failures occur during use), to staff development through in-service training, demonstrations, and so forth. The specialist also consults with the principal and teachers to develop strategies for translating curricular needs into library media center goals and activities.[24]

Curriculum design is an aspect of instructional consultation that involves the library media specialist working as a team member with teachers to plan and implement units of instruction. It requires an awareness of curriculum, collection content, instructional design, and research and reference techniques. Chisholm and Ely suggest that the library media professional should be identified at the beginning of a project and should help locate existing sources and help create materials where none exist. This pro-active professional must assume new responsibilities and go beyond traditional roles.[25] Stripling urges "direct involvement by the SLMS [school library media specialist] in the curriculum at all stages from needs assessment to evaluation."[26] Loertscher's taxonomy places instructional design at levels nine and ten and considers it to be of high priority when structuring library media programs and services.

Curriculum design is perhaps the most time-consuming and involved function performed by the library media specialist. High levels of district and school support are essential for this aspect of instructional consultation to occur. When it is an ongoing activity, optimal educational outcomes are the results.

Instruction

The instruction role occurs at levels three through eleven on Loertscher's taxonomy. This role requires the library media specialist to use the principles of effective teaching when instructing students in library media skills and research techniques, helping students develop an appreciation for good literature, and assisting students and teachers in locating and evaluating information. The teaching of library media skills is basic to the educational process for it is these skills that give students the power to successfully manipulate the information explosion.

In the past, a literate person could be educated in relatively few years and could utilize the acquired information over a lifetime without great need for an expanded base of knowledge. Today the body of knowledge is increasing at a phenomenal rate and no one can hope to acquire all the information needed for a lifetime during the brief span of time spent in formal schooling. One can hope, though, to learn how to learn, one aspect of which is the ability to access data bases and locate information from a variety of sources. Library media skills are the keys to lifelong learning and must be a major objective of the educational community.

Information Provision

Providing information is the raison d'être of a library media center. Consequently, the library media specialist has the responsibility of making resources available. This role assumes greater proportions as technology expands the options for meeting this task.

One of the most important aspects of providing information is the casual, unstructured contact between the library media specialist and the student or teacher (levels three and four on Loertscher's taxonomy). As individuals need assistance, they request help from the specialist. The way the specialist handles such requests may have a lifelong effect on the individual. As an educator, the specialist must know how much information should be given outright and how much should be left for the student to seek out independently. Too much help and the student does not learn to use materials properly; too little help and the student becomes discouraged and does not seek further assistance. Of course, the specialist must be very well acquainted with the collection to provide this necessary service.

Literature

Many library media specialists believe that providing quality literature and teaching young people to appreciate it is one of the most important objectives of the library media program. They view as a flaw in *Information Power* that literature is included only peripherally. It is alluded to as part of the mission and challenges, "The library media program is seen as vital for motivating young people to select and read printed materials with pleasure, to reach for more complex levels of expression and comprehension, and to evaluate these experiences critically." *Information Power* includes literature as a part of the teaching role by encouraging students "to appreciate the value of literature and recreational media in the life of an educated society." But the practical issue remains. The concept of literature as a key aspect of the library media specialist role is not developed. Even in the delineation of the teaching role, the importance of literature is primarily ignored. "[R]ecognition of the pleasure and fulfillment to be derived from using various media for both information and recreation" is one of the major concepts of the teaching role stated, but "recognizing" is passive rather than active and by including literature only as one type of media, the message is further diluted.

Summary

The school library has evolved from a simple book collection to a multifaceted media center. Today's philosophy of library media center management is based on total integration of media into all areas of the curriculum. Though national standards have become increasingly specific, there is still little uniformity in library media centers across the nation.

District support of library media programs can be assessed by examining six criteria: (1) written district philosophy; (2) school library media funding; (3) distribution of block grant funding; (4) school library media center staffing; (5) library media center facilities; and (6) district support staff. At the school level, support can be judged by evaluating (1) the written philosophy; (2) scheduling; (3) teacher attitudes; and (4) the collection.

The library media specialist, working under guidelines established by the district and the school, strives to create a program that is an integral part of the ongoing curriculum. National standards serve as a yardstick for measuring progress. As both educator and librarian, the library media center specialist's responsibilities include instructional consultation, instruction, and information provision.

CHAPTER 2

Policy Writing

A quality library media program is built on the firm foundation of a written philosophy and specific procedural policies. Without a written framework, decisions tend to be made by circumstance and chance. When the purpose and function of the library media center are not defined, teachers and administrators may have differing expectations of what the service comprises. When there is no common, agreed-upon point of reference to serve as a guide, crises and recrimination often occur. Written statements provide direction and guidance not only for the library media specialist, but also for all those who interact with the school library media center. When questions arise, the philosophy and policies provide the answers.

Every school library media center should be supported by a written mission statement and philosophy, as well as written selection, circulation, weeding, scheduling, and operating policies. These documents should be approved through the official channels in the school. This authorization allows the library media specialist to perform the job freely, confident that the needed support network is in place.

Policies specify the services offered by the library media center and delineate day-to-day functions and responsibilities. Because policies tend to reflect the current implementation of a library media center's philosophy, all policies should be reviewed each year. This evolving nature of policies can help achieve the higher levels of service espoused in the philosophy. This chapter will discuss the eight steps of policy writing illustrated in figure 1. Later chapters will discuss specific elements of each document.

When entering a new school, the library media specialist must first determine whether written documents governing the library media center exist. If the previous specialist did not have written and approved documents, the new specialist must begin the process. When written policies do exist, they should be read carefully to determine if they mesh with the philosophies of the district, the school, and the incoming specialist. The decision must be made whether to retain the policies as they stand or make changes. As it becomes necessary to write or rewrite some or all of the policies, these eight steps should be followed.

Eight Steps of Policy Writing

1. Research

Most school districts have a written manual detailing their long-term philosophy and the short-term policies and procedures they use to enact it. It is valuable to read all parts that

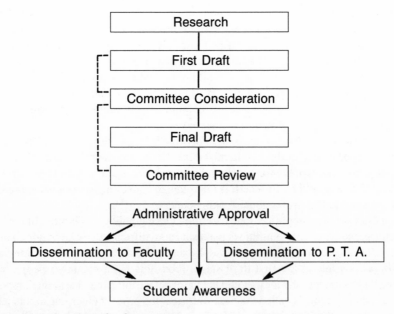

Figure 1. Eight steps of policy writing

are pertinent to students and curriculum as well as those directed especially to library media centers.

The school may also have its own manual; however, if no written guidelines exist, meeting with the principal to discuss school philosophy and policies will provide a starting point for the specialist in developing library media center guidelines.

When the library media specialist is acquainted with district and school philosophies, policies, goals, and operations, the library media center's philosophy and policies can be adapted to this existing structure.

It is imperative that the library media specialist be aware of specific school situations and the structure of the school community. Special programs for students (i.e., mentally and physically handicapped, gifted and talented, or nontraditional), special curriculum offerings, and class groupings or scheduling are all areas with which the library media specialist must be familiar before attempting to write policies. Other considerations include library media budgets, staffing, and the extent and currency of the existing collection.

Researching all of these factors takes time, and is essential before beginning to write. The specialist must allow sufficient time to get a feel for the climate of the school and a sense of the school's attitude toward education and library media service.

2. First Draft

When the research step has been completed, it is time to take pen in hand and verbalize abstract concepts. The elements of a mission statement, philosophy, and specific policies are detailed elsewhere in this book, but some general guidelines apply for writing all first drafts.

The first draft serves as an opportunity for the library media specialist to put into words the philosophy and ideas gained from university classes and experience. It is a time to reflect on services and to define those services in a positive manner.

The documents are intended to enhance understanding of the library media program as the specialist conceives it. They should not be written in library jargon, but in plain English that is readily understood. Clarity of thought is essential. Each document should be short (one-half to one page) and to the point. Long, rambling statements obscure rather than clarify the information being conveyed.

The format of the documents is as individualized as the specialist. They may be written as a paragraph, outline, or itemized list. Content is the prime consideration, not style. One final caution: the format should be consistent, spelling should be checked for errors, grammar should be correct. It is important to convey a professional approach and that means producing professional-looking papers.

First draft writing should be done carefully. Once a policy reaches the library media committee, the nature of committees makes it more difficult to make major changes. It is important, therefore, that the philosophy and policies be as clearly written and as specific as possible at the first draft stage. From this point on, other people will be reading the documents and they should get the exact meaning the library media specialist intends. Although this is called the first draft step, the product emerging at this juncture will probably be the third, fourth, or fifth draft. No one except the library media specialist knows how many times the first draft was revised.

3. Library Media Committee Consideration

Only when the drafts are completed to the satisfaction of the specialist should they be given to a library media committee. A committee should be created if one does not already exist. This committee is an important constituency in policy writing as the members are the first school group to see the documents and can serve as a sounding board.

Membership on the committee should consist of all library media specialists in the school with one being designated as chair. The principal or assistant principal (preferably the person responsible for curriculum) should be included, and several teachers should be appointed. Even in a very large school, four to five teachers are sufficient. If there are too many teachers, the committee becomes unwieldy. Teachers should be chosen from diverse subject areas to provide the broadest representation possible. At the elementary level, teachers should be selected from both primary- and upper-grade levels with one person representing special programs. At the secondary level, teachers should be chosen equally from academic and nonacademic subjects and should have an interest in library media programs and services. A parent, appointed by the principal or the library media specialist, adds an important dimension to the committee. An optional member of the committee may be a student representative.

When the committee first meets, its discussion should be focused on the documents and should not digress to unrelated topics. Each member of the committee should receive a copy of the drafts before the meeting.

Consensus on all items in the philosophy and policies should be achieved if at all possible. If consensus is impossible, it may be necessary to rewrite the disputed item after the library media specialist confers with an administrator.

Ample time should be provided for discussion, and committee members should be made aware that they will see the finished product before it is distributed. The committee should also be informed about the dissemination process.

4. Final Draft

The next step involves rewriting the documents to reflect the changes agreed upon by the library media committee. Revision should be straightforward as it is basically a matter of adding and deleting information; the form and style probably will not change.

5. Committee Review

Committee review at this point is primarily a courtesy gesture. If the committee reached consensus it will probably not reject the final draft. The revised documents should be photocopied and distributed with a request that each committee member read them, initial to indicate approval, and return the revised copies to the chair. A meeting is not needed; however, if substantial disagreement results, the committee must be reconvened and the process reverts to step 3.

6. Administrative Approval

If the principal of the school has not been a member of the library media committee, he or she should be given a copy of the policies. A conference should be arranged to discuss any questions the principal might have. This is an important step as the principal is ultimately responsible for everything relating to the school. A principal who is informed and consulted in advance will be more supportive if problems arise.

If the school has a board or council that forms a governing body, the philosophy and policies must be presented for its endorsement as well.

7. Distribution to Faculty and Parents

Every teacher in the school should be given a copy of the mission statement, philosophy, and policies to keep for reference. A discussion during a faculty meeting will help resolve questions and clarify issues.

Presenting these documents to the parent/teacher organization gives parents an understanding of the library media program and is an important aspect of school public relations. Although the documents may remain unchanged over several years, teachers and parents change. Each year the library media specialist should alert new teachers, new administrators, and parent groups to the existence of the policies and should reinforce them with veteran teachers on a regular basis.

8. Dissemination to Students

Informing students of the library media center's mission statement and philosophy will help them understand the value of the center for their education and personal growth. They must also be informed of circulation and operating policies so they will know what is expected of them when using the center.

At the elementary level, it is best to conduct an oral discussion of the policies and rules with each class. A large poster listing the rules and procedures should be located in a prominent place in the library media center.

At the secondary level, a copy of the rules should accompany a discussion, preferably during orientation. If the school has a student handbook, circulation and operating policies of the center should be included.

Summary

A written mission statement and philosophy, and the selection, weeding, circulation, and operating policies required to implement them, are the essential documents needed to support every library media program. It is important that the philosophy and policies reflect district and school philosophies, the school situation, and recommended practice.

When documents must be written or revised, using the eight-step process provides a sequential approach. The eight steps of policy writing are (1) research, (2) first draft, (3) committee consideration, (4) final draft, (5) committee review, (6) administrative approval, (7) faculty and parent dissemination, and (8) student awareness.

CHAPTER 3

Library Media Philosophy

The school library media philosophy provides a framework for the library media program. It articulates beliefs, concepts, and attitudes about learning and is the foundation on which the goals and objectives of the program are developed.[1]

The philosophy is an outgrowth of the mission statement, which defines the purpose of the center, its goal, and the patrons served. The mission statement is concise and direct, as can be seen in the Salt Lake City school library media mission statement:

> The School Library Media Center provides curriculum support, research guidance, enrichment through literature appreciation, and other learning experiences to the students, faculty, staff and patrons of the school community. The Center fosters a positive environment that encourages inquiry and discovery through the use of organized, accessible resources. The School Library Media program teaches students to be independent lifelong seekers of knowledge who are capable of information retrieval and who value libraries and learning.

It is important to articulate the mission of the library media center before developing a library media philosophy.

The philosophy statement is based on professional knowledge of library media services coupled with each school's individual concept of the library media program. Thus, the statement should express unique as well as universal characteristics of library media centers.

Ideally, the library media philosophy should be incorporated into the written school philosophy. Where this is not the case, a separate document must be developed. Most important, the philosophy should be thoroughly understood and accepted by the school community so that the entire staff is working toward the same goals.

The philosophy reflects any restrictions limiting improved practice, but also provides the means to guide the program toward the optimal levels of services identified by Loertscher: formal planning, instructional design, and curriculum development.[2] The program may be functioning on a low level of Loertscher's taxonomy, but the philosophical abstraction provides a bridge to the desired level. The philosophy outlines the present and future scope of the program. The development of an optimal library media program is dependent upon a carefully stated philosophy.

The terminology used in writing the philosophy conveys meaning to policies and programs. Frequently used terms, such as library media, instructional design, or curriculum development, are intended to lead the school community toward a common understanding of the purpose of the library media program and its role within the educational mission of the school.

The philosophy statement stems from the values a school aims to instill and the educational goals it seeks to achieve. The contribution of the library media center to the school's mission should be generally stated.

The specialist's own perception of library media service, is incorporated into the philosophy statement. This promotes a favorable climate for communication and improved understanding of the library media program.

This chapter will discuss the factors that contribute to the development of a library media philosophy, the components to be incorporated in the philosophy as illustrated in figure 2 and the basis for developing an operating policy.

Contributing Factors

District Philosophy

As discussed in chapter 2, each school district has a philosophy of education expressed in a written statement. It is important that the building-level library media philosophy complement and support that of the district. If the philosophy portrays a program based on teaching, service, and support, teachers and administrators will be encouraged to think of the library media program as an integral part of the educational program.

A crucial aspect of the district's philosophy is a realistic correlation between goals and funds. A "pie-in-the-sky" statement ignorant of financial fact will remain a list of empty platitudes, whereas a realistic statement will be more likely to actually meet the district's educational goals.

School Philosophy

The state of the school-level philosophy will affect the library media program just as the district's philosophy does. A newly assigned library media specialist will need three to six months to grasp the situation. In this period, as well as during annual reviews, the

1. Purpose of the library media center
2. Patrons to be served and extent of service
   a. Students
   b. Teachers
   c. Support staff
   d. Parents and community
3. Evaluation standards
4. Evaluation standards for library media specialists
5. Library media committee
   a. Composition
   b. Role
6. Philosophical supporting statements
   a. "Library Bill of Rights" and "Access to Resources and Services in the School Library
      Media Program: An Interpretation of the Library Bill of Rights"
   b. "The Students' Right to Read"
   c. Support of the U.S. copyright law

Figure 2. Philosophy outline

specialist should strive to openly communicate with all school staff members in order to accurately prepare for writing the philosophy statement.

Curriculum

The curriculum of the school has important implications in philosophy writing. The first consideration is the age level of the students. Younger students, say those under ten, will obviously use the library media center differently than will high school students. The center focusing on younger students may emphasize literature appreciation and reading enhancement while one for older students may emphasize independent use of a wide range of materials.

Academic orientation of the school also affects the philosophy of the library media center. A magnet high school for the performing arts will relate its philosophy to preparing students for performing arts careers, while a traditional high school will have a philosophy developed around meeting a wide variety of student needs and interests. In the specialized school, philosophy is more intently focused in a single area, while in a traditional high school, focus must include consideration for college-bound, vocational, and business students.

The teaching methodology advocated within the school is the third implication of curriculum. All library media philosophies should acknowledge the importance of meeting individual needs of students, but a school practicing the concept of individualized instruction will need to carry the concept further and indicate the extent of commitment to this teaching methodology. If the school has a practice of homogeneous or heterogeneous grouping of students, library media philosophy may need to reflect this concept.

Elements of the Library Media Philosophy

Delineation of Purpose

The philosophy must clearly enunciate why the library media center exists. The most generally accepted purpose of a center is to teach students to use the resources that meet their curricular and extracurricular needs. How this is done and to what extent will depend on the circumstances of the given school. Only the specialist, acting in concert with school representatives, can decide what purposes the library media center should fulfill.

Eligible Users

The philosophy must explicitly state who may use the resources of the library media center in order to avoid hasty decisions when someone other than a student asks to borrow materials. Procedures for circulating materials to designated patrons are specified in the circulation policy; the philosophy merely states who may have borrowing privileges. Users may be:

Students. Students in the school are the first priority of a school library media center. The facility exists for them and it is their reference, research, and leisure-reading needs that must be met.

Faculty. Faculty members, of course, must have full access to the center and its services and teachers should be encouraged to make extensive use of materials within the context of curriculum. Service to faculty may include a professional collection of materials. A professional collection is required in a fully functional center that meets the extended needs of the faculty, but budget constraints do not always permit this element. A philosophical statement may support the concept while acknowledging budget limits. Curriculum manuals, an important element of a professional collection, are usually available at no cost through district and state offices and can serve as a basis for a rudimentary professional collection.

Staff (support personnel). The extent to which support personnel may utilize the resources of the center depends on the philosophical stance. Aides and other paraprofessionals who work with students may need the same access to materials as teachers. This use is normally directed by a teacher and is specifically related to the curriculum. The direction is less clear with other support staff. Use by staff members for personal needs is an additional consideration.

Parents and community. Parents of students may come to the center requesting materials. This raises an issue related to the purpose and function of the school library media center. Whether or not members of the community at large are granted circulation privileges is a definite philosophical consideration in small communities without adequate public library facilities. Private schools within the community are normally restricted from using public school resources and vice versa.

Evaluation Standards for the Program

Accreditation is a legitimate evaluation tool for secondary schools and some elementary schools and is conducted by a regional association. Most accrediting institutions conduct an intense on-site visit at regular intervals and require detailed status reports in intervening years. How much importance is attached to substandard evaluations depends on the accrediting body; however, maintaining the minimum status for continued accreditation is a priority for most schools.

Most states have established standards for evaluating library media centers. Meeting the state guidelines may be mandated by the state board of education or the evaluation may be used to provide focus and direction for growth. In either case, state standards play an important role in guiding library media development and philosophy.

In some districts, standards have been established that must be met. As is true of state evaluation tools, district evaluations can help the library media specialist compare what should be with what is.

The AASL/AECT 1988 guidelines, *Information Power*, can help the specialist compare the local program with high-service programs. Using these qualitative standards as a measure of evaluation, the specialist can initiate a planning process that will address the specific needs of the school curriculum.[3]

Unfortunately, evaluation tools rely primarily on quantitative standards rather than qualitative ones. Reference is made to the number of books, pieces of equipment, or space available for various functions. Seldom are there evaluative criteria for measuring the level of service and the quality of materials. It is difficult to formulate a tool that will evaluate these subjective qualities. Therefore, it is important that the specialist and the principal develop an assessment of the qualitative aspects of the program and that reference to this evaluation be made in the philosophy.

Philosophical recognition of short-term goals should be included. These goals need not be enumerated within the philosophy but recognition should be given to their yearly development by the specialist and the principal.

Library Media Specialist Evaluation

Demand for accountability of the professional staff in schools has grown in recent years. Casual evaluation by the principal is no longer sufficient. Instead, detailed evaluations by the principal and library media director are becoming standard practice. Personnel evaluation methods, therefore, should be mentioned in the philosophy statement.

State or district guidelines may exist that establish evaluative criteria for personnel. These guidelines usually will be more general than specific, as are the *Information Power* guidelines, for it is impossible to pinpoint specific accountability measures away from the local site. District-developed assessment tools often are directed to the teaching staff rather than to specialized roles. In situations where all personnel are required to be evaluated using the same tool, library media specialists should be careful to include reference to an assessment that is more job specific.

A job description written at the local level is a good basis for evaluation and should include all relevant aspects of the job that can reasonably be performed, given the parameters of local conditions. Similarly, the job description and accountabilities of support staff for the library media program must also be addressed.

Finally, the library media specialist needs to set individual goals that will be evaluated at the end of the year. Specific assessment procedures, however, need not be listed in the philosophy statement.

Library Media Committee

The composition of the library media committee should be designated in the philosophy as this body plays an important role in the development and implementation of policies and programs. Typical members would be the library media specialist(s), teachers, the principal or an assistant principal for curriculum, and a parent. Student representation varies among schools.

The role of the library media committee should be stated in the philosophy. Whether the committee will make policy, approve policy, or uphold policy are important distinctions that must be made. All members of the committee need to be aware of the role(s) they are being asked to assume. The certification level of the staff will determine, to a great degree, whether the committee is advisory or participatory and the extent to which it will be involved.

Philosophical Statements of Support

To support the local school library media philosophy, a statement recognizing salient documents should be included. Those philosophical statements most often included are the ALA Library Bill of Rights, the accompanying "Access to Resources and Services in the School Library Media Program: An Interpretation of the Library Bill of Rights," and "The Students' Right to Read" (National Council of Teachers of English). If state or locally approved statements exist, they should be appended. These statements may be attached in full to the written philosophy, but should appear in the document itself by title only.

Specific support of the copyright law of the United States should be included. With the advent of easy duplication of print matter, video and audio recordings, and computer software, it is essential that the philosophy acknowledge that the law be upheld.

Operating Policy

An operating policy details major elements of the philosophy and other policies that affect student use of the center. Its purpose is to convey to students, teachers, administrators, and parents the day-to-day procedures of the library media center. This policy is very detailed and should be carefully reviewed each fall to ascertain that it is current and relevant. Figure 3 illustrates the five parts of an operating policy.

1. *Days and hours of service.* Specifying the days and hours of service is essential. Recommended practice suggests that the center be fully available at least thirty minutes before school and forty-five minutes after classes end; during all lunches, recesses, or class changes; and every day that school is in session. This amount of service would be ideal, but there may be limiting factors, such as staff size, school hours, and the extent to which others outside the school setting are encouraged to use the facility. Another factor that may need to be considered is whether students are encouraged, or indeed allowed, to remain in the building after school. In some situations, bus schedules determine when most students arrive and depart. Beyond the need for student use, before- and after-school hours are important for interactions with teachers. This may be the only time when teachers and the library media specialist can get together to plan and design instructional units.

2. *Materials, equipment and services.* The operating policy lists the types of materials available, including books, filmstrips, video tape recordings, and computer programs. Those materials circulated from a district or regional center should be noted in the operating policy. Equipment housed in the school is listed. Services provided for students, such as individualized reference assistance, are defined.

Any limitations in materials and equipment, whether due to inadequate staff size, collection, or budgets, should be noted.

3. *Summary of circulation policy.* The key points of the circulation policy are briefly summarized (see chapter 4).

1. Days and hours of service
  a. Days of service
  b. Hours of service
    (1) Lunchtime, recess, class change
    (2) Before and after school
2. Materials, equipment, and services
3. Circulation policy summary
4. Student use of the center
  a. Independent use
  b. Class use
5. Behavior guidelines

Figure 3. Operating policy outline

4. *Student use of the center*. Whether students use the resources of the center on an individual or a class basis is distilled from the scheduling process (see chapter 5).

5. *Behavior guidelines*. Students need to know the behavior expected of them when they are in the center. The policy of strict silence that gave librarians the stereotyped "Shh!" image is no longer advocated. However, because a library media center is a place for learning, some restraints are necessary to keep it from becoming solely a social area. Specifying expected behavior eliminates questions regarding what is acceptable.

Factors relevant in determining behavior guidelines are the ages of the students, the number of students that will be in the center at one time, and the expectations of faculty and administration.

Summary

A written library media philosophy serves to underline the value of the center. This statement documents the thrust that the program will have within the school. Elements that influence the writing of a philosophy are (1) the district philosophy, (2) the school philosophy, and (3) the curriculum. The philosophy statement includes (1) the purpose of the center, (2) eligible users, (3) program evaluation standards, (4) specialist evaluation standards, (5) the library media committee, and (6) supportive philosophical statements.

An operating policy provides guidelines for the day-to-day operation of the library media center. This policy specifies (1) days and hours of service; (2) materials, equipment, and services available; (3) circulation procedures; (4) student use of the center; and (5) behavior guidelines.

CHAPTER 4

Circulation

Providing students and teachers with curriculum-related materials is the most pervasive component of curriculum involvement and the one most visible to patrons and the public. To successfully accomplish this function, materials must leave and return to the center in an orderly fashion.

Although some items, because of high demand or cost, will seldom or never circulate, a general policy of closed stacks and no circulation directly conflicts with the philosophy of a school library media center. Therefore, because most materials and equipment will circulate, some type of system must be established. The circulation system serves two purposes—to track items that have been borrowed, and to evaluate the use of materials and equipment.

Tracking materials and equipment is necessary for managing the collection. The honor system may work with a small classroom library of paperbacks, but it will not be successful when dealing with a library media collection containing thousands of items.

Circulation records are essential when performing a needs assessment for equipment purchases and collection development. With circulation statistics at hand, it is a relatively effortless task to determine subject areas in high demand and pieces of equipment with high usage. This data can be analyzed and used as a basis for selection (see chapter 6).

Too many school library media centers have circulation systems that have evolved without careful planning and thought. A circulation policy must result in a standardized approach so that the duties of assistants may be discharged uniformly. This chapter will focus on development of a circulation policy, the elements of a circulation policy, two basic circulation systems, and the problems of theft and loss.

Developing a Circulation Policy

The circulation policy will directly affect every user of the library media center so it is important that the policy be developed carefully. There are four factors to consider.

1. *Collection size and quality.* The number of items in the collection may influence the loan period for materials. A small collection may require a short circulation period to allow the greatest student access to limited resources. Likewise, a collection with major deficits in specific subject areas may need a short circulation period so that students have more opportunities to find needed materials. Conversely, a school with a large collection and multiple copies of high-use items may have a longer circulation period. Collection size becomes irrelevant if a large part of the collection does not meet curricular needs and should be weeded (see chapter 10).

2. *Grade level.* The age of the students served is very important when setting circulation time and establishing overdue procedures. Younger students generally check out materials for only a week or two. A longer circulation period is not needed for using the majority of items and students may forget what they have checked out. High school students, on the other hand, usually need a longer circulation period with two weeks, a term, or a quarter being the norm.

3. *Number of students.* The more students in the school, the larger the collection must be to meet their information needs. *Information Power* suggests that a high service program in a high school of 500 to 1,000 students will have between 16,320 and 25,939 volumes or between 19 and 29 book titles per student.[1] The ratio of students to number of items is directly related to reserve books, reference materials, and periodicals, and is therefore a crucial influence on circulation policy.

4. *District policy.* District policy occasionally may predetermine the ways in which materials circulate, but this is usually left to the discretion of the individual school. District policy is more apt to control fines, specifically when and how fines may be imposed and accounting procedures to be used when money is collected.

Elements of a Circulation Policy

The circulation policy comprises all the procedures necessary for the orderly dissemination of materials, as outlined in figure 4. Written, standardized methods for checking out materials, handling renewals, and controlling overdue and lost items are crucial for efficient operation of the library media center.

Circulation Parameters

The varying nature of library materials, the community being served, and interlibrary loan requirements all affect circulation policy. This section describes the differing loan periods needed for the wide variety of items available for circulation, and discusses how circulation policy must provide for lending outside the confines of the school.

1. Circulation parameters
   a. Collections
      (1) General book collection
      (2) Paperback books
      (3) Teacher collection
      (4) Reference materials
      (5) Reserve materials
      (6) Periodicals
      (7) Audiovisual materials
      (8) Audiovisual equipment
   b. Community
   c. Interlibrary loan
2. Check-out procedure
3. Renewals
4. Overdue materials
5. Lost materials

Figure 4. Circulation policy outline

Collections

When students check out items from the library media center, they must know when to return them. It would be much simpler if the specialist could set one circulation cycle and have it apply to all materials. Unfortunately, this is not feasible. Each element of the collection (i.e., general books, reference items, audiovisual equipment) requires a different loan period.

General book collection. Fiction, nonfiction (including biography), and story collections constitute the largest part of a center's book collection. These books generally are read from beginning to end and the reader requires enough time to complete the entire book. As a rule, books in the general collection circulate for between one week and approximately nine weeks (the length of a one-quarter term). When the circulation time is only one to two weeks, a renewal policy is needed. Teachers often are given open-ended return dates for books in this category.

Paperback books. Most library media centers circulate paperback books in the same manner as books in the general collection. Other centers, however, utilize a paperback exchange where students may take one paperback and leave another in its place without signing for the book. If this system is used, it is important for the library media specialist to regularly assure that the appropriate guidelines are followed.

Teacher collection. Books and materials purchased for teacher professional development are usually located in a separate collection. They circulate for as long as the teacher needs the item or until another teacher requests it.

Reference materials. Reference materials include encyclopedias, dictionaries, atlases, and other books that are used for a short time to find specific information. Because these are high demand items used relatively briefly, usually they should not be allowed to circulate. However, older encyclopedias and reference works may circulate on a short-term basis when there are a sufficient number of newer volumes to handle daily use.

Reserve materials. Reserve materials are items held at the circulation desk. They are placed on reserve by a classroom teacher for a specific assignment or by the specialist because of high possibility of theft (*Masterplots* is often on reserve for this reason). When teachers request that materials be restricted to reserve status, they may set the guidelines for how long the materials will remain on reserve and the length of the students' borrowing period. Generally, reserve books circulate for one class period with overnight use permitted after school.

The decision to place books on reserve beyond teacher requests is somewhat controversial. It is essential to consider seriously whether the best possible use of a book can be made when it is on reserve and must be requested. Too often, students do not realize that the reserve materials exist and hence lose access to valuable resources. With minimal effort, one can encourage access to these materials by utilizing catalog card *Reserve* cover slips, which are readily available from library supply houses. These plastic covers are easily placed over cards in the catalog and will signal to patrons that there is something special about that title. A printed listing of current reserve items can also increase access to and utilization of these materials.

Periodicals. Periodicals present difficult circulation decisions. Some are used frequently, while others remain untouched. If periodicals are circulated, they are prey to rapid deterioration and the selfish removal of individual articles. Solutions to this problem include obtaining periodicals with permanent value in micro format or providing access to a data base that has complete text possibilities. There is no perfect solution and much depends upon the school and its resources (see chapter 11).

Audiovisual materials. Whether audiovisual materials may be checked out to students or only to teachers depends on district and school policy or practice and, especially, on the extent to which the curriculum is individualized. Ideally, all materials should be available to students with audiovisual materials circulated much the same as books, thereby providing students with materials best suited to their learning styles. Unless the center has a large collection of audiovisual materials and adequate equipment, it may not be practical to provide this service to students at all times. Many schools do not permit audiovisual equipment to leave the grounds and, obviously, certain items normally will be restricted. Video players, 16mm projectors, record players, and opaque projectors are too expensive or too bulky for students to borrow. It then becomes impractical to check out films, records, and so forth. When students have compatible equipment at home (i.e., video/audio players or computers), questions of equity and copyright arise if students are accorded borrowing privileges of these items. In general, teachers should be encouraged to use audiovisual materials in their classrooms and "wet" carrels (equipped with electrical outlets) should be set up to facilitate student viewing and listening in the center. Students may be permitted and encouraged to take audiovisual materials to the classroom with teacher supervision.

Audiovisual equipment. As mentioned, ramifications for allowing students to borrow audiovisual equipment are extensive. Circulation policy for equipment, as a rule, will determine how teachers are provided with the equipment they need for classroom use. Not all equipment will circulate for the same length of time. In determining how long teachers may keep equipment items, it is necessary to have an accurate inventory and assessment of need. Some items, such as cassette tape recorders and overhead projectors, should be available in sufficient numbers to allow a teacher who frequently uses them to have one in the classroom all year. Filmstrip projectors, 16mm projectors, and video players will seldom be plentiful enough to permit one per classroom. An equitable system for getting these items to teachers when needed must be established. Equipment may be delivered and picked up each day from a central location, usually the library media center, or it may be kept in a wing, department, floor, or pod and informally borrowed by the teachers during the year. Secure storage is a necessity for equipment with high theft potential: video recorders, cameras, cassette tape recorders and microcomputers.

Two caveats exist regarding equipment circulation. First, accurate records must be kept that report where each item is at all times, regardless of its circulation period. A check-out card or form can be signed when the teacher takes possession of the item and initialed on return of the equipment. A wall chart or peg board can be used to visually track equipment. A computer is very efficient in tracking equipment, provided the circulation information is entered with each transaction. Any of these systems will reduce chances for losing track of expensive equipment.

The second caution relates to students who may deliver equipment to and from classrooms. This can be a dangerous task and some necessary precautions may need to be taken to avoid accidents (see chapter 12). Permanently bolting larger pieces of hardware to equipment carts decreases the possibility of equipment shifting and falling onto a student and makes theft more difficult.

Community

In some small school districts, the school library media center also serves the community. When this occurs, patrons from the community must be made aware that school needs have greater priority. Generally, only the regular circulating book collection, including paperbacks, is made available to community patrons. Other materials may be used in the center, but may not be removed from the premises. Two weeks is a standard circulation period.

Interlibrary Loan

A school library media center may be included in a district interlibrary loan program or it may be affiliated with a county or state library system network of resource sharing. CAVALIR in Virginia, the Metropolitan Washington Library Council, and the Northern Area Network of Pennsylvania are examples of public library/school library media center networking.[2]

As with community use, interlibrary loans generally pertain to the general book collection and, occasionally, periodicals and audiovisual materials. Generally the loan period is fairly short so that students and staff within the school are not inconvenienced should the materials be needed for instructional purposes. Materials may be photocopied for interlibrary use; however, copyright laws must be followed. It is recommended that a copyright warning statement be stamped on any photocopy being provided. Library supply houses stock rubber stamps with appropriate messages.

Check-Out Procedure

Student and teacher check-out of materials should be routine. Students at the secondary level may need to show proof of identity and provide their homeroom number. Elementary students sign their names (at least first name and last initial) and room numbers. Check-out may be on an honor system or be supervised by an adult paraprofessional, volunteer, or student aide. The major concern is that students know what steps to follow in the process of checking out an item (see "Circulation Systems" below).

Renewals

Renewals are usually permitted when circulation periods are relatively short and if there has not been a request for the title by someone else, which would precipitate a hold being placed on the item. Whether or not the user must have the item to be renewed in hand is a question to be addressed in the policy.

Overdues

Overdue materials are a perennial concern in school library media centers. There must be a statement about when materials are to be returned, but policy should not be so stringent that students avoid borrowing materials or so lax that they do not return them for months at a time.

The due date is set for a reasonable period of time during which most students should be able to use the item and return it. When materials are not returned on time, there may be allowable excuses, such as illnesses, school-related activities, or absences authorized by a parent.

Whether to charge fines is a philosophical issue that must be decided. Recommended practice suggests that fines not be levied until students are at the secondary level. The purpose of a fine is not to raise money, but to provide a penalty that will be an incentive to return materials on time so that others may have access to them. Fines are not the ultimate solution to stopping the late return of materials. Indeed, fines create work for the library media staff and anger the students who must pay them, but so far no one has come up with a better deterrent to late returns at the secondary level. Fines usually are fairly low for materials circulating from the general collection and higher for reserve books and other items of high demand. The days that will be counted in computing the fine must be designated. Schools generally charge only for days when school is in session, excluding weekends and holidays. A maximum fine limit should be set. Half of the replacement cost is considered fair.

When materials are overdue, notices must be sent to remind students to get the item(s) back to the center. This is a practical measure as the student may have forgotten that the item is out unless reminded that it is overdue. A computer can generate such notices or pads of preprinted notices can be purchased from a library supply outlet. Lists of students in a teacher's homeroom can be prepared and the library media specialist may request that the teacher remind the students to return the materials. If teachers are asked to do this, some type of follow-up should let the teacher know if the student returned the materials. Posted lists may also keep students aware of their obligations. At some point, the home must be notified of serious delinquencies. This can be accomplished through a telephone call or a written notice.

Whether or not fines are charged, there will be a few students whose refusal to return materials becomes a serious problem. Policy should designate at what point borrowing privileges will be withdrawn until the student returns or pays for overdue materials.

Lost Materials

Some books that are overdue are actually lost and this will eventually be apparent to the student and library media specialist. Almost all centers require students to pay for lost materials; the question is how much should be charged. The item will have to be replaced, but there are no hard and fast rules that establish an equitable amount to charge.

There are four standards used in establishing a charge for a lost item. All are feasible and the decision may be based on the economic status of most students or the library media budget for materials or both. The four bases for charge are (1) cost of the item when it was purchased, (2) current replacement cost, (3) replacement cost plus processing cost, and (4) prorated cost to allow for wear.

Some lost or damaged materials may no longer be available and cannot be replaced while others may be dated and no longer relevant. Policy should avoid stating that all proceeds from lost books will be used for exact title replacement.

Once a lost book has been paid for it is no longer a circulation problem, but a matter of selection policy. However, lost books do not always remain lost. Some will eventually be found and returned. Policy must predetermine the question of a refund for the borrower who paid for the item. Four options exist for handling this situation.

1. The entire amount paid is refunded.
2. The fine that would have accumulated is deducted from the refund.
3. The fine that accumulated prior to payment for the loss is subtracted from the refund.
4. The item has been replaced and the student has paid for the item; therefore, the item is returned to the student.

The fourth option is seldom used in school library media centers as priority usually is placed on availability of materials and replacement is a fairly slow process. It may be considered as an option if the item is found after a year or more.

School library media center circulation policy must also address the consequences that occur when a student loses an item and does not pay for it. This decision is intertwined with district and school policies and should not counter those policies. Prior to formulating this aspect of circulation policy, the specialist must be conversant with those established criteria.

Schools use different penalties in this situation. None are intended as punitive measures, but rather as incentives to encourage students to return materials and be responsible for school property. Before assessing penalties, a time period for reasonable return or remuneration must be established. When the student does not comply within this reasonable time, additional measures are required.

A loss of library media borrowing privileges is a standard procedure in many schools. The student is not barred from the center and, indeed, has full utilization privileges within the center; however, the student may not check materials out of the center.

Other restrictions may include holding report cards for parent pick-up, losing early registration privileges, forfeiting nonessential course changes, or holding yearbooks. The important criteria for establishing penalties for irresponsible students are that no restriction be legally invalid or violate district or school policy.

Finally, hardship cases must be considered when levying charges for lost materials. Students should have the option of substituting work in the center for payment or of paying for the item in small installments. When these alternatives are agreed upon, no further penalties are incurred. A reduced assessment in certain circumstances may also be considered. Again, the key is legality and existing district and school policy.

Circulation Systems

Manual Systems

A manual circulation system relies on a card file for maintaining records of materials that have been checked out and who has borrowed them. Every book and audiovisual item has a check-out card with its accompanying card pocket and date-due form. The pocket is placed in an easily accessible spot, which, in books, is usually inside the front or back cover. Placement of cards for audiovisual materials depends on local practice, size, packaging design, and storage space. Placing the pocket and card inside the box lid is a common practice for sound filmstrip sets and kits, for example.

Both card and pocket are marked with identical data to ensure an exact match when the item is returned after use. Included on both card and pocket are the author's name (books only), the title, and an accession number or copy number (see chapter 8).

The student or teacher who wishes to check out an item removes the card from the pocket and signs her or his name and homeroom number. The card and date-due slip are both stamped or marked with the date the material must be returned, and the patron leaves with the item. The check-out card remains in the center and is filed in the appropriate card file. When an item is returned, the correct card is located in the card file, data on the card and pocket are checked to ensure an exact match, and the card is reinserted into its pocket.

Advantages

1. Familiarity. Most students and adults are comfortable with the card system. They have had experience in using it and know how to proceed independently. Student aides, having used this system for checking out their own materials, can easily be trained to oversee the process.

2. Cost. A card circulation system is a low-budget operation. Cards, pockets, and date-due slips are inexpensive and the only essential item is a card tray, usually made of inexpensive wood. Date stamps are an asset, but not a necessity. Preprinted pads make writing overdue notices less time consuming, but homemade notices duplicated on a photocopier or ditto machine will serve as well. Not essential, but highly recommended, is an alphabetizing card sorter, which facilitates filing large numbers of cards.

3. Reduced new material preparation time. Fully processed books, whether purchased from a supplier or obtained through district cataloging, arrive with a pocket and card already prepared. The school adds the accession or copy number and the book is ready for circulation. Audiovisual materials are usually purchased with card sets, but seldom include a pocket. Preparing a pocket is a relatively easy task that can be done by a student or volunteer in minutes.

4. Check-out speed. As each student signs his or her own card(s) at check-out time, the process requires only seconds to complete. The cards are put in a designated spot to be filed at a later time. It is possible to collect cards from an entire class in a minute or less.

Disadvantages

1. Time. A card system involves repeated handling of the check-out card every time the item is circulated. Initially, the student or an aide, volunteer, or paraprofessional must stamp or write the due date on the card and place it into a daily file. At the end of the day, circulation records are completed by counting the cards for each Dewey classification. The cards are then arranged in some logical fashion (author, title, accession number) and filed behind a tabbed index card marked with the date due (1–31), specific room numbers, or teachers' names. When the item is returned, the card file is searched to locate the correct card, which is then replaced in the pocket. If cards are filed under a teacher's name or room number, this should be marked in the book (the date-due slip is a good place) to facilitate location upon return.

Materials that are not returned on time cause additional card handling. The cards for all overdue items are pulled daily, weekly, monthly, or quarterly and notices are written. This may involve alphabetizing the cards by student name to compile an accurate list of all items owed by a single student. After this is done, the cards are re-sorted and refiled.

Even more time and handling are required when a student leaves the school permanently or when someone needs to locate an item that is checked out. The only way this information can be obtained is by checking every card. This can be so time consuming that some specialists do not bother to check.

An option for schools with highly mobile populations is to use a dual card system. A card is created for each student and is retained in an alphabetical file at the circulation desk. Each time a student checks out materials the transaction is recorded by listing the borrowed items and date due on the student's card. Alternatively, two identical circulation cards are created for each book in the circulating collection. One card is then filed by the student's name, and the other by due date. The alphabetical file of students would be consulted to determine the items checked out to that student; this file would require updating with each student transaction.

2. Probability of error. A card system relies on the accuracy of the individuals who file the cards and return the cards to the book pockets. Each transaction increases the possibility of human error. When student aides assist in the process, the possibility of error increases because many more individuals are working in the system daily.

Errors made by returning a card to the wrong pocket are often difficult to trace. If the item with the wrong card is on the shelf, the problem is readily corrected. However, if another student has checked out the item and signed the mismatched card, there is no quick solution. There may be even more serious problems if a mistake has been made and a book is lost. These problems arise most often with duplicate titles. Careful instructions to students and staff about the necessity of carefully checking cards and pockets will help reduce these mix-ups.

Computer Systems

A computerized circulation system is an excellent application of the computer's management function. A computerized system provides a quick and efficient record of which materials are checked out and has the capability of reporting all materials checked out to an individual.

There are many excellent commercial circulation systems available that can be used with a microcomputer. These programs are steadily growing and improving. This discussion will be limited to microcomputer systems, as the decision to use network mainframe or minicomputers is seldom in the hands of the school specialist.

Selection of software must precede selection of hardware and should be based on how well the program meets the defined specifications. Loertscher advises that the library media specialist should list all functions desired, find a system that meets those specifications, and check with other users to see how well the system works for them and how much support service is provided by the company.[3]

Purchase of the following components is necessary for a computerized circulation system:

Library circulation software
Microcomputer
Floppy disk drives, or hard disk drive, or 3 $1/2''$ disk system
Light pen or bar wand
Printer

Although floppy disks are less expensive than a hard disk, most users find that a diskette-based system is relatively slow and efficiency is reduced by the need to change disks frequently. A hard disk drive will handle all functions easily and quickly.

Automated circulation systems have certain common elements. Every item in the collection is identified with a bar code sticker. Each bar code is matched in the computer to the author, title, and copy number of the item. Each borrower is assigned an identifying bar code number and this is also entered into the computer.

To check out an item, the identifying code for the circulation program is first entered into the computer. The patron's identification card is entered into the computer's memory by passing a light pen over the bar code. (Cards may be kept at the circulation desk, if preferred.) Materials are then checked out to that student by passing the light pen over each item's bar code.

The due date is entered into the computer each morning and the computer automatically records this date with each transaction. The due date should be stamped or marked in the item being checked out so that the student has a visual record of when the item is to be returned.

When the item is returned, the command for the materials return program is entered and the light pen is passed over the bar code on the item. The computer finds this record in its memory and clears the item for subsequent checkout by another user.

Advantages

1. Accuracy. Circulation records are more accurate than with a card system as there is little chance that an item can be mistakenly assigned to the wrong individual. It is impossible to check out an item until the previous circulation data have been cleared.

2. Time. This is the advantage most often cited for installing a computerized system. Items are checked in and out in seconds and information about individual patron records, individual titles, and overdue materials is available immediately. Not only is the information quickly retrieved, but it can be printed and ready for distribution within minutes. There are no cards to file and flags can be coded into many programs to alert the library media specialist that a student has overdue materials or that someone has placed a hold on an item.

3. Data statistics. Not only is the time-consuming compilation of daily, monthly, and yearly circulation records handled by the computer with ease, but the variety and amount of statistics that may be generated is greatly expanded. A check of computer records can readily provide vital information for collection development, for example (see chapter 6).

Disadvantages

1. Cost. Establishing a computerized system is definitely more costly than using a card system. Hardware is a major consideration but is not the only costly item. A software package must be purchased that will provide the services desired. Hardware and software are the major financial considerations, but there are additional factors to bear in mind. First, there must be a safe, adequate source of electrical power near the circulation desk. Second, supplies such as bar code labels and computer paper must be included in the budget.

2. Time. Time spent on the circulation process will be significantly reduced with an automated system, but before this saving can be realized, someone must enter all the information. Some software companies will input a shelf list onto floppy disks. This is a great time-saver provided the shelf list is 100 percent accurate and money is available to pay for the service.

Lacking outside service, many specialists spend their entire summer, often without pay, entering the information. Students with good typing or keyboard skills can assist with the data entry. By running a printout and checking for errors, corrections can be made by the specialist in a short period of time. Information input is a time-consuming task that should be completed prior to implementation. It is possible to enter the data during the check-out procedure, but this slows down the circulation process considerably.

Another factor to be considered is how students check out material. If entire classes check out materials at once, the time needed to use the light pen on each item may be as time consuming as collecting cards.

3. Computer failure. There will come a day when the computer will fail, but a back-up system solves the problem. A written log of items checked out with appropriate bar code numbers permits the information to be entered into the computer when it is again functioning. If floppy disks are used, a back-up copy must be made each day to avoid disk failure. Hard disk systems often use videotape or floppy disks for back-up.

Before deciding to install a computerized system, the specialist should take a serious look at these disadvantages and decide if they can be overcome. Although many repetitive data manipulation and analysis operations have been successfully computerized, further criteria must be applied to determine if the method will be profitable.[4] If funds are available and there is sufficient staff and time to prepare materials and enter information, the process of computerizing the check-out system will probably be highly successful. If there are significant stumbling blocks, it may be necessary to continue using the card system while trying to overcome the problems.

Theft

Loss of materials due to theft varies greatly from school to school, but it is a rare library media center that never experiences it. Some thefts are intentional, others are accidental. For example, a student is studying in the center and is surrounded by stacks of materials. The bell rings, personal belongings are gathered, and the student leaves, unaware that some materials that should have been checked out or left in the library media center are included.

Books, periodicals, and vertical file materials disappear most often, mainly because of their size and portability. After all, there isn't much use for a filmstrip without a projector, and it is difficult to conceal a kit or large picture.

Grade level is related to the problem of theft. Fewer thefts occur with K–3 children than with older students.

One factor conducive to a high rate of theft is the number of exits from the center. In schools without walls it is common to find the library media center filled only with old books—new ones disappear off the shelves as if by magic.[5] Library media centers contained within walls but having multiple exits suffer the same problem, although they do have the advantage of being locked after hours. The concept of total accessibility is wonderful in theory but unrealistic in terms of building a viable permanent collection.

Security Systems

One way to control the problem of theft is by installing a security system. This has been shown to reduce losses by alerting staff when someone tries to leave without checking out an item. A detection system relies on defined exits and is not feasible in an open-concept center.

The two most commonly installed systems are Checkpoint® and 3M Tattletape®. Both require application of an electronically sensitive device that is easily deactivated at the circulation desk. If a student attempts to leave the center without having the item desensitized, an audible signal sounds.

The Checkpoint method involves placing a 1^1/2″ to 3″ sticker in a visible location on an item. This can double as a date-due label (a small sticker is applied when the item is checked out) or can serve as an identification label. Special labels are available for cassette tapes and hard tags are available for equipment. Checkpoint also permits a by-pass system that does not require materials to be desensitized, but rather passed behind the circulation desk to avoid the electronic system. The by-pass is less applicable in schools than in public libraries.

The 3M Tattletape system requires insertion of a small, electronically sensitive tape into a book spine or other inconspicuous spot on the item. When exiting the center, the student passes through a barrier that locks and sounds an alarm if unauthorized material is being removed. The newer 3M Echotag® system uses small markers and a nonbarrier detection device.

Before investing in a security system, consider all costs involved. Normally, the greatest expense will be installation, but some schools may need to remodel exits to accommodate the system. The initial purchase of security tapes or labels will be somewhat costly; new additions will be a minor expense. Staff time to insert tags and labels and to oversee student or volunteer help must be considered. If a specialist is operating a center single-handedly, this will be a major consideration. Another consideration is the purchase of nondesensitizable identification tags for reference items. This variation assures that reference items do not circulate inadvertently. Schools, however, need to consider what happens to their reference materials when they are replaced with newer editions. Most library media centers place their older items into the circulating collection and, if permanently sensitized identification has been used, considerable effort may be needed to remove it and replace it with desensitizable identification.

A security system will not eliminate all theft-related problems. In fact, it may increase student determination to "beat the system" or create havoc by deliberately triggering the alarm. Student pranks to set off the alarm are usually a short-lived phenomenon as the novelty wears off. The greatest single problem that results is the mutilation of periodicals and reference books when students tear out articles or pages they need.

Additional Strategies

Other strategies to combat loss and damage can be used by schools that have a security system as well as by those that do not. Students need to have "ownership" of the materials. The collection should be seen as belonging to the students, not the specialist.

Requiring students to show identification when checking out materials prevents fictitious names from being used. A file of picture identification cards kept at the circulation desk can be useful with both card and automated systems.

The fewer materials there are on reserve or in reference, the less temptation there is for theft. For this reason, as well as for philosophical reasons, materials restricted for center use only need to be selected carefully.

A photocopier is valuable in reducing theft. If copies can be made for a nominal fee or at no cost, the need to "borrow" noncirculating items will be reduced. Microform copies of periodicals are an additional deterrent to theft of research-related materials (see chapter 11).

An alert specialist and staff will be aware of the climate in the center and can develop strategies to meet individual problems. While no single strategy will totally eliminate theft and damage, the more approaches tried, the lower the theft rate will be.

Summary

The circulation system is an integral component of library media center operation and serves to track as well as evaluate the use of materials and equipment. A circulation policy standardizes the process. The policy is determined by (1) collection size and quality, (2) grade level, (3) number of students served, and (4) district policy. Elements included in the policy are (1) loan periods, (2) check-out procedures, (3) renewals, (4) overdues, and (5) lost materials. Circulation can be handled manually with check-out cards or it can be automated with computers. The problems of theft and damage can be reduced by using purchased security systems and by such internal strategies as student "ownership" of materials, required identification, few noncirculating materials, photocopiers, and microforms.

CHAPTER 5

Scheduling

Effective functioning of a school library media center is dependent to a great extent on scheduling. To facilitate maximum use by students and teachers, it is essential that there be a plan for who will use the center at what time and for what purpose. A carefully thought out procedure to handle scheduling and a policy based on curriculum needs are required for every library media center.

This chapter will focus on scheduling theory, factors affecting scheduling, four types of schedules and their implications, the elements of a scheduling policy, and steps to follow in implementing the chosen schedule.

Scheduling Theory

School library media centers have the definitive function of teaching library media skills; it is this function that makes a scheduling plan essential. It is the teaching function, along with instructional design, that differentiates the school library media center from the public library. With the body of knowledge expanding at an ever-increasing rate, it is imperative that schools teach students how to locate and use the available knowledge. A well-articulated scheduling plan gives students the opportunity to gain these skills.

A schedule has three primary purposes. The first is to assure equitable access by channeling students in numbers that can be supported by the physical facility, the material resources, and the staff.

The second purpose is to help the library media specialist know what to plan in order to teach the desired skills. A lesson must be planned if it is to be effective and the specialist needs advance notice of who will be using the center and for what purpose in order to develop a substantive lesson.[1]

The third purpose of the schedule is to help the specialist assess center use. The number of different classes scheduled into the center is one indication of the extent to which the center is being used. If the schedule shows large periods of time when the center is not being used, it is a signal to the specialist to work more actively with teachers to plan units that will bring classes into the center.

Scheduling Considerations

Before a library media schedule can be designed, it is important to recognize that what takes place while students are in the center has empirical, philosophical, and curricular implications. Class time spent in the library media center should be directly related to teaching or reinforcing library media skills, and applying those skills to classroom work. This can occur in large- or small-group instruction. Students may learn new skills, review skills previously taught, or practice skills in supervised or independent activities. All of these components have their place in the instructional process and should be part of library media teaching strategies.

Class time in the library media center should be considered an integral part of inculcating an attitude of lifelong learning. The library media program should be designed to help students process and use information and develop skills in selecting materials that meet their information and leisure time needs. Time spent in the library media center should be directly related to students' educational growth.

The more involved the classroom teacher is in the teaching that occurs in the library media center, the more the concepts taught will be a comprehensive part of the students' educational development.[2] When instructional design is an ongoing aspect of library media specialist/teacher interaction, library media instruction is most effective.

Learning theory emphasizes the importance of integrating library media skills into the curriculum. The four basic premises of optimal learning have direct bearing on the teaching of library media skills and, hence, on the schedule that is developed.

1. Optimum learning occurs when the student has a need to learn. Ideally this means that the teaching of any library media skill will coincide with a related classroom assignment. In order to do this, the library media specialist must be actively involved as a team member with the classroom teacher in planning and implementing units.

2. Optimum learning occurs when the lesson is individualized. Teaching methods and materials should be varied to be responsive to students' learning styles. Obviously, the library media center is the logical site for individualized learning. The variety of materials provides access to information in a multiplicity of print and nonprint formats.

3. Optimum learning occurs when there is opportunity for practice of the newly acquired skill. Upon being taught a specific skill, the student should have time to use that skill during the same class period. Practice, to be effective, must relate to reality. A work sheet may give practice in using a skill, but it will be far more effective if it is relevant to the ongoing classroom curriculum rather than an isolated activity.

4. Optimum learning occurs when a newly acquired skill is reinforced periodically. Once the student has mastered the skill, there should be frequent opportunity to use it and there should be adequate supervision to verify that the skill was indeed learned and that it is being used correctly. This means that the reinforcement period should follow the initial teaching period fairly quickly, a day or two later at most. If reinforcement does not occur for a week or two, there will be a significant loss of the original teaching, which will have to be repeated.

These four principles of learning and their part in the school's philosophy have great relevancy in developing a library media schedule. When library media scheduling is built on effective principles of learning rather than teacher convenience, significant educational outcomes are realized.

Beyond the philosophical and theoretical considerations involved in schedule development are some practical factors. Realistic assessment of these factors is necessary if the schedule that is developed is to succeed.

Library Media Center Staffing

Library media center staffing is a critical concern in planning a schedule. The number of professionals and paraprofessionals assigned to a center will determine the amount of time available for working with classes and individuals.

Scheduling difficulty increases when the number of students exceeds the availability of staff. However, time spent in teaching and working with students must be a priority. The areas of television, computer technology, media production, programmed instruction, and technical processes must take second place to instruction, instructional consultation, and information provision. Reduction in teaching time should occur only as a last resort.

Staffing is an important aspect of extended hours service. A single individual cannot open the library media center at 7 A.M., close it at 5 P.M., and be available during all lunch periods. The larger the staff, the more extensive service hours can be.

Class Load

Class size is of special concern as it affects the teaching process and, hence, the time that needs to be scheduled for a given purpose. The larger the class, the longer the time period required to complete a given teaching segment. This is especially relevant if individualized instruction is used. In addition to the amount of time devoted to initial instruction, large classes require more time for supervised practice as it takes longer for the library media specialist to check student comprehension, give needed one-on-one feedback, and assess progress.

Library Media Center Size

The space available in the library media center determines the number of students that can be served at any given time. Chairs and tables, circulation area, reference area, stacks, and conference rooms are factors to be considered as a schedule is developed. For a school with 500 students, *Information Power* recommends a minimum of 1800 square feet for entrance/circulation, small group, conference area, multipurpose room, and stacks. Seating area is additional.[3] Using *Information Power* as a guide, it is possible to gauge the number of students who can use the center simultaneously.

A large center, one that conforms to or exceeds the guidelines, may have enough room for several classes to visit simultaneously. In this situation, guidelines are necessary to direct the purpose of classes scheduled into the center. Generally, instruction in library media skills can be given effectively to only one class at a time. Even though two classes may wish to have the same instruction, teaching will not be as effective with such a large group. When space permits, however, classes may simultaneously use the center with one class receiving instruction and the other working independently under the guidance of another library media specialist or teacher.

Individuals using the center independently should be permitted access at all times as theory recommends. An extremely small center may preclude this practice as the room may be so congested that additional students will interfere with the teaching process. In that case, time must be scheduled for independent student visits.

Grade Level

Elementary schools have different scheduling considerations than do secondary schools. In the elementary school, it is important that time be allowed every day for students to select and check out books. Secondary students have time between classes or other time that may not be available to elementary students.

Secondary classes are usually controlled by a formal time structure. At the end of a class period, a bell dismisses students. In developing a library media schedule, a secondary schedule will match designated periods. Time flexibility occurs only in the number of days scheduled for a specific class. Elementary classes are more flexible for the most part. An elementary schedule can be developed around the purpose for the visit and the time needed to complete the instructional task.

Other Factors

The parameters of scheduling options may be restricted by mandates beyond the library media specialist's jurisdiction. District policy and procedure may explicitly delineate how the library media center is to be scheduled. This may be advantageous or restrictive, but it must be adhered to. It is difficult to change a restrictive directive issued from the district level and this should not be attempted by an individual new to the system. Normally there is a process through which district procedures can be changed. It is important to develop a plan cooperatively with supervisors and other specialists and to gain the principal's support within this framework.

Negotiated teacher contracts may specify how library media schedules are to operate. This may be very restrictive if a contract was negotiated that defines students' library media time as a teacher preparation period. To alter such a contract, it is necessary to generate concern among teachers and teacher representatives who will lobby for change.

Another constraint placed on the development of a library media schedule may come from the building administrator. The principal may have very definite ideas ranging from very flexible to very rigid about how a library media center should be scheduled. A newly assigned administrator may have preconceived ideas about how the center should function. It is easier to change a new administrator's viewpoint, if it is restrictive, than to change that of the board of education or a teacher's negotiated contract. A library media specialist who can validate the educational philosophy behind the recommended schedule can often bring about changes successfully.

Schedule Variations

Four library media center schedules are typically found in schools: traditional, block, open, and flexible. No single schedule is universally workable, nor is it necessarily recommended that one be used exclusively in any school. Combining aspects of several plans is often the best action.

Traditional Scheduling

The oldest, and least recommended, schedule is the traditional one that brings all classes into the library media center at least once a week for skills, materials check out, and related activities (see figure 5). The center is tightly scheduled with all available times

Time	Monday	Tuesday	19____ – 19____ Wednesday	Thursday	Friday

Figure 5. Traditional schedule

allocated for classes and professional work. Students are admitted to the center only with their class or before and after school.

The traditional schedule still exists in schools across the country although it is losing favor to schedules more consonant with current learning theory. It has survived as a scheduling option because tradition and existing practices are difficult to change.

Traditional scheduling is seldom used in secondary schools because it is not responsive to the needs of the curriculum and the school schedule. A class in library science may exist in secondary schools with students scheduled into the center on a regular basis, but this schedule rarely precludes the availability of the center for use with other classes or individuals.

The primary use of traditional scheduling is in elementary schools. Even here it is less frequently used in schools with over 600 students, as there are not enough hours in the week to schedule everyone and do all of the professional work required.

Schools that use a traditional schedule seldom have an adequate ratio of professional and support staff to students. Generally, they are staffed by a single professional (in some schools this is a part-time position) with minimal, if any, clerical help. The concept within the school is that library media is another class for students, similar to art, music, or physical education.

Traditional scheduling is the least flexible of all the schedules and, due to the limited amount of access it allows, is the least responsive to student and teacher needs. It should be implemented only when other alternatives are not viable. The goal of a specialist should be to move toward a less rigid approach. "Any functions that restrict or interfere with open access to all resources, including scheduled classes on a fixed basis, must be avoided to the fullest extent possible."[4]

Advantages

Although the disadvantages far outweigh the advantages, there are educational reasons for schools opting to use this schedule.

The traditional schedule gives every student an opportunity to use the library media center on a regular basis. This has public relations value as parents are aware of the library media center and its weekly effect on their child. Because of the regularity of the schedule, the curriculum can be structured to cover the requisite skills. Children are encouraged to select leisure reading materials during their weekly visit and, as a result, all children have extended reading materials at hand.

While working with a class, the specialist is free from interruptions. Interruptions by individuals and teachers can totally disrupt a teaching lesson. If the library media center is closed during classes, this problem does not exist.

Teachers like the traditional schedule because it provides them with a preparation period. They often come to view this as released time and appreciate the break it gives them.

Disadvantages

The theoretical and philosophical implications of the traditional schedule are so removed from current theory and philosophy that there are few valid reasons for maintaining it. The disadvantages are counterproductive to good practice and it is difficult to imagine a truly justifiable reason for continued use of the traditional schedule.

Students may not use the library media center except when their class is scheduled; therefore, they do not have access to materials when they are needed. Students who are able to read quickly may not have the opportunity to exchange books as soon as they are ready.

Teachers may view their library media time only as a break from teaching and not accord the program the legitimacy it deserves. Although they appreciate the time available for their own use, they do not take time to consider what is happening to their students during this period. "Out of sight, out of mind" may apply. In addition, there is no time for the library media specialist to work individually with students and teachers.

Block Scheduling

Block scheduling, illustrated in figure 6, brings students into the library media center for several consecutive days at intervals throughout the year. These times may be prearranged at the beginning of the school year or the schedule may evolve as instruction needs arise. The blocked time is used for intensive teaching of library skills or research and is most effectively done in conjunction with a classroom assignment. The library media schedule changes each week as different classes are targeted.

This type of schedule is often used in secondary schools. A subject teacher confers with the library media specialist(s) about the purpose for bringing the class into the center. The specialist teaches skills to meet that purpose or prepares to assist students with research projects when they are adequately trained to search independently.

This schedule is often used at the elementary school level in grades 4–6. Primary grade students, K–3, generally are not learning skills dependent on daily continuity, but need planned interaction at regular intervals. Again, best results from this schedule are produced when there is cooperative interaction between the classroom teacher and the library media specialist and the skills taught are applicable to a definite classroom assignment.

Block scheduling does not address the needs of individual users. Good practice dictates that individuals always are welcome and, given requisite center space, this type of schedule can accommodate individuals concurrently with classes. Indeed, individuals must be allowed daily access in order to select and check out materials if there is no weekly selection period.

Advantages

The block schedule is a good step forward from the traditional schedule. Students are more apt to remember and utilize the skills taught during their block time as reinforcement occurs consecutively. As teachers schedule their classes when the skills are coordinated with a classroom assignment, there is a need to learn and to practice the application of a skill. Vacation and special event days can be taken into account when the class is scheduled so that interruptions are minimized. This lessens the gap between the initial teaching, reinforcement, and use that often occurs when students must wait a week or more in a traditional schedule.

Disadvantages

The block schedule is preferred over the traditional schedule, but it does not meet all needs. Although it addresses two aspects of learning theory—need to learn and opportunity for practice—it does not automatically provide for individualization and periodic reinforcement may or may not occur.

Date _____

Time

Teacher and Subject

Purpose

Figure 6. Block or flexible schedule

Block scheduling is not appropriate for kindergarten through second or third grade. The skills taught in these primary grades need practice and reinforcement at regularly spaced intervals.

Students at all grade levels have large time gaps between their scheduled use of the center. The weekly contact needed to build appreciation and interest is missing. Literature tends to be neglected as class periods emphasize research and skills. This aspect of library media service should not be ignored.

A student who is absent during the blocked time may completely miss the concept taught. This can create problems not only in library media skill attainment but also in the fulfillment of classroom assignments based on the assumption of skill mastery. Special arrangements should be made to provide make-up opportunities when this schedule is implemented.

Open Scheduling

Open scheduling refers to a plan that has no formal arrangements for the use of the library media center. Students come and go as they need access to the resources of the center and as the classroom teacher permits. Entire class visits do not occur.

This schedule is often used in schools architecturally designed to have complete access from one area to another. The library media center is located in the middle of these schools with classrooms positioned as satellites. "Schools without walls" emphasize the totality of the learning process and the library media center serves as the hub of learning activity. The open plan may be used in a traditional setting, but the existence of walls and the separation of individual classrooms make it less likely that the free flow of movement will occur.

For open scheduling to succeed, there must be total teacher and administrator support and a commonly shared philosophy of individualized learning. The open schedule must evolve out of the school's need for such a plan. It cannot be mandated by the specialist or principal, but must arise to meet the perceived needs of teachers and students. When agreement is reached that the open schedule best meets the needs of the school, and the administrative philosophy supports the schedule, the library media specialist coordinates implementation. Integration of the library media center into the curriculum, encouraged when the open plan is implemented, supports the four maxims of learning theory and involves the library media specialist at the highest levels of Loertscher's taxonomy.

It is not easy to develop a fully functioning open schedule. Unless there is real commitment and dedication to the concept on the part of the teachers, the center may become a place of inactivity with minimal student interaction. The specialist must constantly promote the use of the center and must be aware of all units being taught in order to prepare for student requests for materials and services.

Total involvement of the library media specialist in the curriculum is the epitome of recommended practice. However, it does not come without a price. Staffing levels must be commensurate with those schools having above-average, high-service programs as identified in *Information Power,* the 1988 guidelines. Unless there is adequate staff support, a library media specialist will burn out quickly. Support staff is essential to handle production, clerical work, processing, and circulation when the library media specialist is totally committed to teaching and curriculum development.

To support the open schedule concept, a large collection of materials is required. When all students in the school are doing individualized work, they must rely extensively on library media resources rather than on textbooks. To meet this demand, up-to-date books and audiovisual materials must be available in sufficient numbers.

Care must be taken to ensure that all students learn the requisite skills for using the resources of the center. It is easy for students to slip through the program without learning the fundamentals of library media use. Individualized learning stations can help meet this need, but careful monitoring is necessary to assure that all students have successfully learned the skills.

Advantages

The open schedule, in its optimum form, has three key advantages that make it a highly desired plan. The center is truly an extension of the classroom and functions as an integral component of the learning environment. The library media specialist is a key teacher and the library media center is truly the hub of learning. The center is available whenever a student or teacher needs immediate information, and students use the center so frequently that they become quite skilled in taking advantage of all available resources.

Disadvantages

Every schedule, no matter how valuable, has some drawbacks. The library media specialist needs to be aware of these so that plans can be made to reduce their negative impact.

With an open schedule, the teaching of skills may be incidental rather than planned. There is no overall curriculum to guide the skills that are taught and there is little time for story telling or discussions of award-winning books, thus limiting exposure to good literature. This is a critical need if school library media programs fulfill the obligation to help develop good readers. Children in grades K–2 are especially at a disadvantage; they may have little contact with the library media center because their curriculum does not provide extensive opportunities for independent interaction.

Control of library media material is often difficult in an open facility, as students are continually entering and leaving the center. Problems of monitoring the open library media center also occur when evening functions are held in the school. Loss of valuable materials is especially serious when security and supervision of the center are lacking because of the physical arrangement.

Secondary school teachers and students, being subject and time oriented, may not fully utilize the library media center and the advantages of the plan may not offset the disadvantages.

One of the most serious disadvantages of the open plan is its lack of responsiveness to whole class use. When students are all working independently, they do not receive the large group instruction that may be beneficial in teaching certain skills.

Flexible Scheduling

Flexible scheduling, the most preferred option, encourages teachers to schedule classes according to project and unit needs. Schedules are arranged to accommodate the time needed to complete the assignment or project (see figure 6). Elementary schools extend the concept of flexibility to include the number of minutes scheduled. For example, a visit planned to introduce students to encyclopedias may last 30 minutes, while the follow-up lesson to reinforce the procedure and give students time to locate encyclopedia information and write short reports may be scheduled for 45 minutes.

During the entire day, including those times when classes are scheduled, individual students may use the center for research and leisure reading. The number of students allowed from any one classroom at any given time may be limited, but the option always exists for this use.

Flexible scheduling is demanding, but it provides optimum service and is consistent with learning theory. Its purpose is to encourage students' use of the library media center on both planned and spontaneous bases.

Adequate professional and support staff is essential for flexible scheduling as individuals need assistance at the same time that large group instruction is occurring. This type of scheduling requires extensive cooperative planning as each period of the day may find classes of different subject areas and grade levels scheduled for different purposes.

Square footage and furniture in the center must be sufficient to accommodate a minimum of 50 to 70 students in a school of 500 or less. This allows room for individual use at the same time that a class is scheduled. The collection must be extensive and current—when large numbers of students are using resources simultaneously, they must have access to the materials they need.

Advantages

Flexible scheduling is most responsive to the needs of classes and individuals. It does not lock anyone into a set time frame and therefore adapts the use of the library media center to changing circumstances. Individuals are not frustrated by closed doors when they want to use the center. Flexible scheduling does, however, provide structure and opportunity for class interaction and large group instruction.

The library media center truly functions as a resource and learning center with this type of schedule. It is responsive to the teaching function and to individual student use of library resources.

Disadvantages

The single disadvantage of the flexible schedule is the possibility that confusion may result from the diversity of activities occurring simultaneously. A lecture or an audio-visual presentation given while other students are studying may not be conducive to student concentration. Individual students may be disruptive if they continually request assistance while the specialist is teaching a lesson. Guidelines that establish how students will use the center independently will help resolve this situation.

Orientation

Regardless of the scheduling plan decided on, time should be reserved at the beginning of the school year for orientation sessions. Yearly orientation sessions for all students are very helpful. Reviewing library media center policies and procedures will refresh students' memories and will set guidelines for use during the year.

In elementary schools using the traditional schedule, orientation usually takes place during the first class visit. Block, open, or flexible scheduling will require the library media specialist to set up a one-time-only schedule that allows each class approximately 30 minutes in the center for orientation.

At the secondary level, orientation usually occurs during English class periods. This is a practical way of reaching the majority of students as most are required to take English classes. A special effort should be made to schedule students in programs such as special education and alternative classes who may be missed otherwise.

Individual class orientation sessions may not be feasible in very large high schools. A video tape recording of the presentation is one solution. It can be shown to students over closed circuit television or viewed on a video player and monitor. The videotape has the advantage of being available for use with students who miss the original presentation.

Scheduling Policy

A library media scheduling policy answers the traditional questions of who, what, where, when, and how. The policy sets the parameters for library media use as it specifically states the ways students will gain access to the resources of the center.

Policy for scheduling is an outgrowth of school and district philosophy and has a definite effect on curriculum. The library media schedule determines the amount and types of interaction that occur between students and the library media center staff. Therefore, the scheduling policy will determine the extent of influence of the library media center within the school and on the students. The elements of a scheduling policy follow:

Who—This element defines who will be scheduled into the center (students) and who will be responsible for arranging the visit (teacher, library media specialist, or both). It also specifies who will be responsible for student behavior, grading, monitoring, and teaching.

What—This element refers to the perceived purposes of student interaction in the library media center. It provides the expected range of usage for browsing, research, reference skills, and literature enhancement. Delineation of what may not be scheduled is appropriate in this section. Too often the library media center is viewed as the catch-all site for activities such as parties, voting, or receptions. Some extracurricular uses are appropriate; for example, faculty meetings offer an excellent opportunity for positive public relations. The fundamental consideration for scheduling activities in the center should be their effect on student use.

Where—Although the obvious site for library media center use is the center itself, occasionally other locations are used. Some concepts may be most advantageously taught in a classroom rather than in the center. This may be a viable option when two or more classes have simultaneous needs and all cannot be accommodated in the center. This element also specifies use of related facilities, such as conference rooms where groups of students may work together on projects.

When—This element defines when students will be scheduled for large group instruction and when they may have independent access to the resources of the center. Time allocations are discussed according to the schedule selected.

How—This final element regulates how the center will be used. It specifies how many large groups can be scheduled simultaneously and how many individual students may be sent from any one class.

Implementing the Chosen Schedule

Regardless of which schedule or combination of schedules the specialist intends to use, the first step must be a conference with the principal. It is essential that the principal and the specialist be in complete accord before writing and implementing policy.

After the policy has been written and approved, the next step is getting the students into the center.

Traditional, block, and flexible scheduling require a calendar or chart on which to record the classes that will be using the center each day. It is important that teachers clearly understand the process for arranging class visits and that they be able to do so efficiently.

Traditional scheduling requires a generic weekly chart with each class being assigned its library media time (see figure 5). The library media specialist may post the chart and ask teachers to select their preferred time(s) or the principal and specialist may assign times. Teacher involvement in designating the weekly time is recommended as the library media time will affect the classroom teaching schedule.

Flexible and block scheduling require daily or weekly calendars (see figure 6) that permit the schedule to evolve according to need. In elementary schools this involves extensive preparation, especially if students in grades K–3 are to have regularly scheduled periods and those in grades 4–6 are to be scheduled according to need. Teachers need to know exactly how to schedule their classes and confirmation of these dates and times is important.

With all types of schedules, some time must be allocated each week for professional work. This may be done before or after class visits are scheduled. The more time that is devoted to instructional consultation, the more time that must be allocated for teacher/specialist planning. Library media centers with sufficient staff will need less scheduled work time than centers without clerical assistance and minimal professional staff.

A scheduling plan must be developed with flexibility to move toward optimal use of the center and its resources. Changes must be introduced slowly; a schedule should not be static and inflexible. Good practice evolves from application of theory to each school with its unique philosophy and curriculum.

Summary

Scheduling is one of the most important structural foundations on which a library media program is built. Without the defining form of a planned schedule, the function of teaching cannot occur. The three primary purposes of a library media center schedule are (1) coordinating available resources and use of the center for student needs, (2) planning, and (3) assessing. There are philosophical, curricular, and practical implications attached to any library media schedule. Four types of schedules are typically used in schools: traditional, block, open, and flexible. Orientation is an important element of any library media schedule. A scheduling policy addresses the basic questions of where, when, and how the students will use the center and is implemented through direct communication with teachers.

CHAPTER 6

Selection

Selection of materials and equipment is one of the most important management tasks of the library media specialist. Selecting the best possible items, given the reality of financial constraints, requires skill and knowledge.

Materials and equipment purchased for the library media center must meet anticipated as well as present needs. Indeed, equipment may remain in use for decades and a poor choice may affect use of materials long after the specialist who made the selection has left the school. Books and audiovisual materials must be selected carefully to fulfill the educational mission of the library media center. They must meet definitive criteria if they are to move off the shelves and into the hands of the users.

The primary consideration for selection must be the needs of those served by the library media center: "Let it be understood clearly that selection never occurs in a vacuum. It is a service for people. Choices of books and other items are always made in terms of those who use, or may use, or should use the library."[1]

Materials are selected to build a strong, viable collection to meet both curriculum needs and student interests. Equipment is selected for use both with materials in the library media center's permanent collection and with materials readily available from outside sources (i.e., 16mm films, videotapes, and other nonprint materials borrowed or rented from a central facility).

Selection is one of the management functions that cannot be delegated to anyone else; the decisions must be made by the professional(s). Delegation to paraprofessionals or volunteers is an abdication of responsibility and an invitation to censorship problems.

This chapter will discuss materials selection in terms of background knowledge, constraints, policy development, selection procedures, and handling requests for reconsideration. Equipment selection will focus on determining needs and allocations in the school.

Materials Selection

Materials are the lifeblood of the library media center. Without materials, the center would not exist. However, materials are not selected for the center but for the students and teachers who will use them.

"A materials selection statement must relate to concrete practices. It should, in effect, provide guidelines for strengthening and adding to the library's collection. . . . It must be a viable, working document which relates to the library's day-to-day operations."[2] In order to make wise selection choices, the specialist must be aware of the greater setting within which the library media center fits. These influences, as well as existing constraints, must be considered prior to policy writing. Policy, when written, contains specific criteria and provides the framework giving the specialist guidance in the selection process. "The educational effectiveness of the library media program is in direct proportion to the quality and appropriateness of the media collection and to the competence and dedication of the library media specialist. A quality media collection meets adequately the developmental needs of the curriculum and the needs, interests, goals, and abilities of the students."[3]

In any discussion of selection, the question of selection versus censorship is bound to be raised. Selection is a matter of choosing, from all of the materials available, those that best fit the needs of the users and identified deficiencies in the collection. The materials are chosen according to guidelines designated by policy and, because care is taken in the selection process, can be defended if necessary. Selection is the process used to put quality materials into the hands of users. Censorship, on the other hand, is the attempt to restrict or prevent access to a specific item in the collection because it or some part of it is offensive to an individual or group. How to handle this problem is discussed later in this chapter.

Influences on Selection

Before beginning the selection process, the library media specialist must consider several factors.

School Curriculum. A prerequisite to the selection process is that the library media specialist be fully informed about the school's curriculum. Knowledge of curriculum means more than just knowing what subjects are taught. It means that the specialist knows the units of study encompassed in the texts and teacher-developed units and understands how to reinforce them with the resources of the library media center. This is crucial if the library media specialist is to become an active partner with the teacher, instead of stagnating as a mere supplier of materials.

School Philosophy. Once again, the school's philosophy of education, as expressed in the library media philosophy, has relevance. The extent to which the library media center is perceived as an integral part of the curriculum will influence selection.

District Policy. District policy and procedure may provide definitive guidelines for selection. If policy and procedures exist at the district level, they must be accorded priority status in forming a school selection policy.

Community Values. Community values do not dictate selection practice, but should serve as one of several guidelines to be used in the selection process. Consideration of these values means being sensitive to subjects that may be of general concern to the community. When selecting possibly controversial materials, it is important to know how they will be perceived by the community and to have defensible reasons for the selection. This concept draws a fine line that should not extend into censorship. It is one area where public libraries and school library media centers diverge significantly in policy.

Ages of Students. The ages of the students who will be using the materials is especially important. A good selection for junior high students will be inappropriate for elementary or high school students. There are very few materials that are suitable for all ages of children; certain basic encyclopedias and reference works are the standard items found at both elementary and secondary levels. An elementary school that includes only primary grades may not have even this commonality. Selection, therefore, must constantly measure an item's level of reading difficulty, content suitability, and the interest levels of the students in the school.

Format. There are many different formats of materials that can be purchased for school library media centers. Books are possibly the only format uniformly purchased by all schools. Audiovisual materials come in a wide range of formats with the same title or content often available as a picture book, filmstrip, sound filmstrip, read-along filmstrip and book, video tape of a filmstrip, 16mm film, or video tape recording. Obviously, it would not be feasible or desirable to have the title in all available formats, so the one or two best suited to need must be selected. Because of cost, most districts make 16mm films available from a centralized source. Other audiovisual items may also be available centrally and this will influence local selection. All materials selected must be compatible with available equipment. Materials should not be purchased on the expectation of acquiring compatible equipment, as this expectation could be frustrated by budget vagaries, leading to the center's possessing dormant materials.

Budget. There is no avoiding the issue of budget. It dictates many aspects of library media service and nowhere is this more apparent than in selection. The number of given dollars will only stretch so far in purchasing materials. The selection policy provides the guidelines for maximizing the potential of the available dollars.

Selection Policy

Having become thoroughly familiar with the school, the library media center and its goals and objectives, and the resources available, the specialist is ready to write a selection policy. "In order to build a library collection, we need a policy that defines the areas in which the library will conscientiously add materials. The collection policy defines not only these areas but also the content and even the format of the materials to be added. Good collection policies avoid generalities whenever possible and focus on specifics."[4] Entire graduate-level courses and books are developed on the subject of materials selection. This chapter does not attempt to cover that ground, but rather builds on that foundation for writing a selection policy and developing management procedures.

Figure 7 outlines the six basic elements of a selection policy: criteria for selection, selection aids, handling recommendations, disposition of donated materials, selection responsibility, and handling requests for reconsideration.

1. *Criteria for selection.* Definition of the criteria used in selecting materials is crucial. It tells others what priorities are considered in the selection process and, more important, sets guidelines to help the specialist make judicious decisions. The concepts of focus, depth and breadth, and balance are primary.

Focus refers to the needs of the students. The curriculum, the amount of independent reference and research work being done, and the extent to which the collection meets extended needs are major considerations in selection.

Depth and breadth take focus one step further and define those areas where material purchases will be concentrated. Depth refers to the number of copies that will be purchased to meet demand and breadth refers to how comprehensively subject areas will

1. Criteria for selection
   a. Focus
   b. Depth and breadth
   c. Balance
2. Selection aids
   a. Professional reviews
   b. Firsthand evaluation
   c. Evaluation standards
3. Recommendations
4. Donations
   a. Integration into the collection
   b. Referral to a classroom
   c. Sale
   d. Refusal
5. Selection responsibility
6. Reconsideration of materials

Figure 7. Selection policy outline

be represented. For example, a policy may state that the collection will contain extensive materials in subject areas covered by the curriculum and representative materials in areas extending beyond the curriculum. Every school has both an explicit and an implicit curriculum and together they cover extensive ground.

Balance within the collection is the third criterion often cited in selection policies. However, "the myth of the balanced collection in a children's department needs to be dispelled once and for all. The range of attitudes available within children's books is considerably narrower than within adult books."[5] Elementary schools tend not to have materials showing all sides of issues nor do they purchase materials on all possible subjects. Secondary schools, however, should retain the concept of balance, especially when dealing with controversial subject matter. If possible, there should be materials available representing more than one point of view. This material may be found in periodicals or other less permanent formats. Social Issues Resources Series (SIRS), a loose-leaf reprint subscription service, is an excellent reference source for current, topical issues. Community values again enter the process when sensitive subject materials are purchased.

2. *Selection aids.* The specialist uses evaluation tools and processes in selecting materials and these should be clearly enumerated. Any professional periodicals used should be listed in the selection policy. Other aids may include district reviews, firsthand evaluations (especially important for nonprint materials), and evaluation standards (accreditation, state, local, etc.).

3. *Recommendations.* Suggestions from teachers and students can be especially valuable in identifying areas of need. These suggestions must be monitored to assure that the recommended material fits the criteria of focus and balance and does not represent a personal bias. Recommendations from teachers for the purchase of nonprint materials are especially important, since these materials are usually used under their guidance. A good rule of thumb is to preview expensive non-print materials before purchase. Knowledge of the school curriculum and teaching styles is essential in evaluating recommendations.

4. *Donations.* Donated materials, usually books and back issues of periodicals, represent an area of selection where delicate decisions must be made. Some gifts fill real needs in the collection while others have no value for the students in the school. Selection

policy should state the options available to the specialist when gift materials are received. Items may be integrated into the collection and, if so, the same standards must apply as they would to any new material being added to the collection. Items that may be more appropriately used in a classroom may be given to a teacher. Selling unneeded items at a book sale is a viable option provided district policy permits such sales. Finally, the specialist should reserve the right to refuse a gift item if the content is unsuitable. The key to successful handling of gifts lies in the options specified in the selection policy. Processing gift materials for integration into the collection is covered in chapter 8. Ensuring that the donor is satisfied is discussed in chapter 13.

5. *Selection responsibility.* The responsibility of the library media specialist to select materials is delegated by the board of education or similar agency. This authorization implicitly entrusts the specialist to select materials that will appropriately represent the board's objectives to the community. In theory this authority is delegated to the building principal, but most principals tend to rely on the specialist's judgment. Despite the specialist's considerable flexibility in selection policy, it is polite to allow the library media committee to review proposed purchases and this procedure should be included in the policy statement.

6. *Reconsideration of materials.* At some point in a library media specialist's career, someone will challenge an item in the collection. Policy, therefore, must be in place to assure that a process is followed and that rash decisions are avoided. Policy should stipulate that a written request be received before initiation of the reconsideration process. Policy also designates the levels of authority through which a request will be handled. These typically include the local school library media committee, a district review committee, the superintendent, and the board of education or governing body of the school system. Specific steps for handling a request for reconsideration are discussed later in this chapter.

Selection Procedures

An approved policy provides the framework for selection of materials. Procedures enable the specialist to manage the selection process efficiently and in the most cost-effective manner. To do this, the specialist must be aware of current collection status, selection tools, systematic ways to handle materials being considered for purchase, and purchase guidelines.

Collection development. Familiarity with the existing collection is essential for selection. The specialist uses several resources to determine the strengths and weaknesses of the collection.

Circulation records indicate which areas of the collection are most used. Records maintained by Dewey decimal system general classifications are not specific enough to be of great value, but will point out broad areas of use. Circulation statistics recording Dewey "tens" categories are much more useful. For instance, heavy circulation in the 500s indicates great interest in science, but a heavy use of the 590s indicates specific interest in animals. The specialist can then assess the 590s and determine if there are sufficient materials available to meet needs. In a similar manner, heavy use of the 500s may not reveal that the 510s (math) have had little circulation. Alerted by more specific records, however, the specialist can review the collection and decide whether low circulation resulted from lack of quality materials or low student interest.

Inventory time provides an excellent opportunity for surveying the collection and ascertaining current status. Weeded materials also flag areas where development may be needed (see chapter 10).

Anecdotal records of unfulfilled research requests document further areas of need. As students need materials for research and cannot find information on a specific topic, the specialist can pinpoint areas of deficiency.

Knowing the condition of the collection is the starting point. In order to develop the collection in a systematic and organized manner, the specialist must have a long-term plan and a strategy for getting there.

For the school library media center, it seems theoretically defensible to divide collection development into three main areas: (1) The building of a basic collection designed to serve a wide variety of interests and needs; (2) The creation of general emphasis areas which contain materials to support whole courses of instruction or numerous units of instruction; (3) The creation of specific emphasis areas that support single units of instruction. [6]

Collection mapping has been proposed as an evaluation strategy for collection development.[7] The strategy begins with an in-depth curricular study: surveying mandated curriculum, textbook adoption cycles, and textbook approaches to curriculum; faculty teaching style, and the expectations of school curriculum developers. A poster is created that graphs the general emphasis collections and the specific emphasis collections. Items from the collection are counted to quantify the number of items available, and student/item ratios are calculated for the general, specific, and total collection. With the quantified data charted, the library media specialist and faculty qualify the identified collections on the basis of diversity of format, currency, relevance to unit needs, duplication, and appropriate level for the students. The chart is displayed for public review of the strengths and weaknesses of the program. The specialist uses the chart to identify purchasing targets, collection development strategies, and budget amounts.[8] The collection mapping and collection development strategy has been shown to be a viable means of evaluating the quality of a collection, which concurs with the recommendations of the 1988 standards.[9]

Selection tools. After a collection development plan has been mapped, appropriate materials must be located. Ideally, the library media specialist(s) would read, view, or hear an item, share this information with teachers, and receive feedback from them on the quality of the material and its relevance to the curriculum and the interests of students. In the real world, this is not possible for most purchases.

One concrete way to determine which items must be previewed and which can be purchased on the basis of reviews is to limit the amount that can be spent for items not actually previewed in the school. For example, an audio cassette costing $29 may be purchased on the basis of its review in a professional journal but a kit costing $189 must be previewed by a teacher or the library media specialist before purchase. Because not all materials can be personally previewed, review journals are a good source of authoritative recommendations for purchase of print materials. Reviews must be read in the context of the journal's reviewing standards and should be balanced by the needs of the collection.

Audiovisual review sources are a tool for selecting titles to be previewed. Many of the same tools that are used for book reviews also contain audiovisual reviews, for example, *School Library Journal* or *Booklist*. Some sources, such as *Science Books and Films* contain specific subject reviews, while others focus on one format, such as *Software Reports; The Guide to Evaluated Software* or *Only the Best; The Discriminating Software Guide for Preschool–Grade 12* for computer software.

Some districts have review centers where materials may be examined firsthand. Browsing through this collection and sampling both print and nonprint items being considered for purchase provides important data. Public libraries in the community may have extensive holdings and can also serve as a firsthand preview source. Additionally, media producers and distributors often make their products available for review, although video and computer formats are frequently exempt from this option at the school level.

Obviously, any item that can be personally inspected can be judged more realistically. Although reading a book is the only way to fully evaluate it, browsing through it quickly and making an educated decision is most practical. While browsing, check the following features:

1. Illustrations (should be clear, properly labeled, and relevant to the text)
2. Index (if nonfiction)
3. Readable print
4. Readability level
5. Clear, concise writing style (paragraphs read randomly will confirm this)

Specific criteria to be considered when previewing audiovisual materials are

1. Content that is factually accurate
2. Visual quality
3. Audio quality
4. Applicability of subject to format
5. Appropriateness for grade level
6. Pace

Discussions with other specialists at meetings or in informal gatherings will often reveal titles that have filled specific needs. A network of peers thus enhances the selection process.

Many states annually bestow awards on books most enjoyed by students and lists of such award winners constitute another selection tool. Because these titles are often nominated by professionals, they, as well as Caldecott and Newbery award winners, should be considered for purchase.

Catalogs, such as those published by H. W. Wilson and Brodart include lists of materials suggested for a specific school level. Catalogs can serve as guides to selection if they include complete bibliographic information as well as review data. Catalogs arranged by Dewey decimal classification are an excellent source for locating materials specifically needed for deficient areas of the collection. Comparing the library media center's holdings with those included in a reputable catalog is one way to determine how well the basic collection correlates to recommended collections developed by others.

Catalogs should not be used as the sole source for decision making. Although catalogs are updated frequently, there is a time gap between the copyright date of an item and the appearance of the item in the catalog.

Periodicals are selected, as are all materials, to meet the needs of students. When periodicals are used to teach research at the elementary and secondary levels, the majority of titles should be selected from the index used. In elementary schools, *Children's Magazine Guide* is an excellent tool. Secondary schools primarily use the *Readers' Guide to Periodical Literature* or the *Abridged Readers' Guide*. CD-ROM and on-line data bases expand the index base and require greater scrutiny of titles for purchase.

Some periodicals are purchased to encourage students to read for enjoyment. These titles may or may not be indexed; their primary purpose is to attract readers.

Selection of periodicals must be compatible with policy standards that relate to students' age and interest level, readability, and appropriateness. Whenever possible, titles should appeal to a variety of interests. Periodicals that meet teachers' professional needs should be selected as well.

Prioritizing Materials for Purchase

Keeping all the selected titles in some kind of logical order is essential so that when the time comes to purchase, it is not necessary to retrace the vital information. There are many ways to keep this information, but two systems seem most successful.

The computer is the most efficient tool for recording and storing data as selection information can be added to a disk at any time. The specialist marks reviews in a journal and a paraprofessional or aide enters the data. For those specialists whose centers lack a computer, a card system can function adequately. As selection occurs, the data is written on an index card (the backs of discarded catalog cards are ideal for the thrifty). A spindle file conveniently holds the cards until selection is in its final steps.

Every item chosen should be given a priority ranking as to how valuable the material is to the collection. This rating should take into consideration how well the item fits the identified needs, how highly it is rated by the reviewing source, and whether cost is comparable to value. A numerical rating system works well.

1 = Highest priority; must have
2 = Valuable to have
3 = Nice to have if money exists

Items that would rank lower than 3 are not included in the data bank. There is no use cluttering files and using valuable time to input information that will not be included on a purchase order. Indeed, with an extremely tight budget, the specialist may decide that only items ranking 1 and 2 will be included for consideration.

If budget permits purchase of all high-quality materials selected, the process is complete when a title is judged to be a good and needed addition to the collection. Few budgets allow this luxury. Instead, the initial selection of titles is only the beginning; winnowing those selections to fit within the budget must follow. This is where prioritization occurs.

The computer list or the index cards may be used to efficiently separate the items being considered into the three previously identified categories. The total cost of the number one priorities is compared to the budget. The titles are analyzed to verify that all remain of the highest priority. Sometimes two titles will cover the same information and there is no reason to have two similar titles. Dividing the number one priorities into identified needs groups will facilitate this process. If money remains after all highest priority items are included, category two titles are scrutinized. The same procedure is followed for those in the third group.

At some point, the total cost will exceed the budget. Items must be further analyzed to determine which should be included for purchase. Although subjective values enter into this decision-making process, the objective data of need fulfillment, quality, and cost effectiveness form the basis for the final recommendations.

A code can be used to identify the selection need the item fulfills. For example, GEO could indicate that the item fills an identified need in geography, FIC in fiction, and USH in U.S. history. The code should be easily recalled and need not be used for all items. Indeed, not all materials selected for purchase fit specific curriculum needs, but those that do should be so noted.

During this prioritizing process, information that will assist the actual purchase should be put into the data base. For books this would be author, title, publisher, and price. Title, producer or distributor, price, and catalog number are needed for audiovisual purchases. Audiovisual orders often go directly to the distributor; therefore, it is wise to include the distributor's address in the file.

The first item of information listed in the computer or on the card file should be the word by which final lists will be alphabetized. This normally is the author's last name or the first word in the title of an audiovisual item. It may be the producer/distributor or the publisher depending on the district's purchasing guidelines.

The review source may be identified. This is especially helpful if, for some reason, the specialist wants to go back to the original selection tool to verify the information. If the item was recommended by a specific individual, noting this will allow the specialist to contact the person when the item arrives.

Requests for Reconsideration

Careful and considered selection of materials according to established policy and procedures reduces the potential for reconsideration requests. It also assures the library media specialist of the item's educational value.

When a reconsideration request is received, the specialist relies on the approved policy to guide the process in a calm, reasonable manner. The steps illustrated in figure 8 are logical and objective rather than reactive.

1. The process begins when a written complaint is received. Patrons making verbal requests are politely thanked, but informed that no action can begin until a signed, written request on the proper form is received. A sample form is reproduced as figure 9. This drastically reduces the number of complaints registered, for many individuals will not take the time and effort to complete the form. Written requests, even if not 100 percent complete, initiate the procedure when they are received.

2. The principal and members of the library media committee are notified that a written reconsideration request has been received. It is best if this is done in writing so that an accurate paper trail exists and there can be no misunderstanding of process. The memo to the principal and committee members reaffirms the reconsideration steps to be taken and includes a copy of the request. The district supervisor should receive a copy of this memo for the record.

When a request for reconsideration is received from a single patron, usually a concerned parent, steps 3 through 5 are followed. Requests received from a group or organization should proceed to step 6 following notification of the principal who is then responsible for referring the request to the superintendent's office. The local committee is notified as a courtesy. The district-level committee becomes the appropriate source for initial considerations when organized groups are involved.

3. A date is set when the library media committee and the patron can sit down together and discuss the material in question. The date should be soon enough that the patron believes that action is being taken, but delayed enough to permit time for all committee members to read or view the material in question and also to allow time for a possibly irate patron to calm down. All involved parties are notified of the meeting date as soon as it is set. In "Policies and Procedures for Selection of Instructional Materials," the

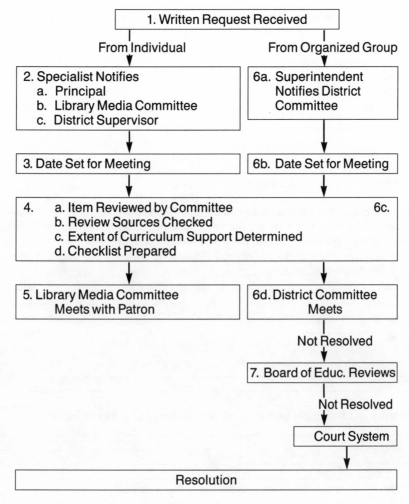

Figure 8. Reconsideration process

American Association of School Librarians recommends that access to the item being reconsidered be preserved during this period.

4. Before meeting with the patron, the specialist checks review sources, books, and lists of recommended materials to verify any recommendations the item received. Checklists, such as those illustrated in figures 10 and 11, pinpoint questions that should be thoroughly reviewed before the library media committee meeting. (If these forms are used, additional comments, recommendations, and signatures should not be completed until after the committee has met.)

5. The meeting of the patron and the library media committee should be structured in a way that lets the patron know that the school staff sincerely cares about the quality of materials available. If the committee believes the item has merit, that belief must be maintained and conveyed. The goal is to help the patron recognize the value of the item and, if the patron continues to disagree, to acknowledge the parent's right to request that his or her child not check out the item. Hopefully, the committee and the patron can reach consensus and the reconsideration request can be resolved amicably.

Request for Reconsideration of Instructional Materials *(Sample)*

School _____

Please check type of material:

( ) Book   ( ) Film   ( ) Record
( ) Periodical   ( ) Filmstrip   ( ) Kit
( ) Pamphlet   ( ) Cassette   ( ) Other

Title _____

Author _____

Publisher or Producer _____

Request initiated by _____

Telephone _____ Address _____

City _____ State _____ Zip _____

The following questions are to be answered after the complainant has read, viewed, or listened to the school library material in its entirety. If sufficient space is not provided, attach additional sheets. (Please sign your name to each additional attachment.)

1. To what in the material do you object? (Please be specific, cite pages, frames in a film-strip, film sequence, et cetera.)

    _____
    _____
    _____
    _____

2. What do you believe is the theme or purpose of this material?

    _____
    _____
    _____
    _____

3. What do you feel might be the result of a student using this material?

    _____
    _____
    _____
    _____

4. For what age group would you recommend this material?

    _____

5. Is there anything good in this material? Please comment.

    _____
    _____

6. Would you care to recommend other school library material of the same subject and format?

    _____

_____   _____
Signature of Complainant   Date

Please return *completed* form to the school principal.

Source: *School Media Quarterly*, Winter, 1977: 113.

Figure 9. Reconsideration request form

Checklist for School Media Advisory Committee's Reconsideration
of Instructional Material—Nonfiction *(Sample)*

Title _____

Author _____

A. Purpose
   1. What is the overall purpose of the material? _____
   _____

   2. Is the purpose accomplished? ____ Yes ____ No.

B. Authenticity
   1. Is the author competent and qualified in the field? ____ Yes ____ No.
   2. What is the reputation and significance of the author and publisher/producer in the field?
   _____
   _____

   3. Is the material up-to-date? ____ Yes ____ No.
   4. Are information sources well documented? ____ Yes ____ No.
   5. Are translations and retellings faithful to the original? ____ Yes ____ No.

C. Appropriateness
   1. Does the material promote the educational goals and objectives of the curriculum of District Schools? ____ Yes ____ No.
   2. Is it appropriate to the level of instruction intended? ____ Yes ____ No.
   3. Are the illustrations appropriate to the subject and age levels? ____ Yes ____ No.

D. Content
   1. Is the content of this material well presented by providing adequate scope, range, depth and continuity? ____ Yes ____ No.
   2. Does this material present information not otherwise available? ____ Yes ____ No.
   3. Does this material give a new dimension or direction to its subject? ____ Yes ____ No.

E. Reviews
   1. Source of review _____
   Favorably reviewed_____ Unfavorably reviewed _____
   2. Does this title appear in one or more reputable selection aids? ____ Yes ____ No.
   If answer is yes, please list titles of selection aids. _____
   _____

Additional Comments
_____
_____

Recommendation by School Media Advisory Committee for Treatment of Challenged Materials
_____
_____
_____

                                  Date _____

Signature of Media Advisory Review Committee

_____   _____
_____   _____
_____   _____

Source: "Policies and Procedures for Selection of Instructional Materials," *School Media Quarterly*, Winter, 1977: 114.

Figure 10. Nonfiction reconsideration checklist

Checklist for School Media Advisory Committee's Reconsideration of Instructional Material—
Fiction and Other Literary Forms *(Sample)*

Title _____

Author _____

A. Purpose

    1. What is the purpose, theme or message of the material? How well does the author/producer/composer accomplish this purpose?

    _____

    _____

    _____

    2. If the story is fantasy, is it the type that has imaginative appeal and is suitable for children? ____ Yes ____ No; for young adults? ____ Yes ____ No. If both are marked no, for what age group would you recommend?

    3. Will the reading and/or viewing and/or listening to material result in more compassionate understanding of human beings? ____ Yes ____ No.

    4. Does it offer an opportunity to better understand and appreciate the aspirations, achievements, and problems of various minority groups? ____ Yes ____ No.

    5. Are any questionable elements of the story an integral part of a worthwhile theme or message? ____ Yes ____ No.

B. Content

    1. Does a story about modern times give a realistic picture of life as it is now? ____ Yes ____ No.

    2. Does the story avoid an oversimplified view of life, one which leaves the reader with the general feeling that life is sweet and rosy or ugly and meaningless? ____ Yes ____ No.

    3. When factual information is part of the story, is it presented accurately? ____ Yes ____ No.

    4. Is prejudicial appeal readily identifiable by the potential reader? ____ Yes ____ No.

    5. Are concepts presented appropriate to the ability and maturity of the potential readers? ____ Yes ____ No.

    6. Do characters speak in a language true to the period and section of the country in which they live? ____ Yes ____ No.

    7. Does the material offend in some special way the sensibilities of women or a minority group by the way it presents either the chief character or any of the minor characters? ____ Yes ____ No.

    8. Is there preoccupation with sex, violence, cruelty, brutality, and aberrant behavior that would make this material inappropriate for children? ____ Yes ____ No; young adults? ____ Yes ____ No.

    9. If there is use of offensive language, is it appropriate to the purpose of the text for children? ____ Yes ____ No; for young adults? ____ Yes ____ No.

    10. Is the material free from derisive names and epithets that would offend minority groups? ____ Yes ____ No; children? ____ Yes ____ No; young adults? ____ Yes ____ No.

    11. Is the material well written or produced? ____ Yes ____ No.

    12. Does the story give a broader understanding of human behavior without stressing differences of class, race, color, sex, education, religion or philosophy in any adverse way? ____ Yes ____ No.

    13. Does the material make a significant contribution to the history of literature or ideas? ____ Yes ____ No.

    14. Are the illustrations appropriate and in good taste? ____ Yes ____ No.

    15. Are the illustrations realistic in relation to the story? ____ Yes ____ No.

Source: "Policies and Procedures for Selection of Instructional Materials," *School Media Quarterly*, Winter, 1977: 115.

Figure 11. Fiction reconsideration checklist

It should be noted that not all items can be defended and poor selection choices may have been made prior to current policy. Although the library media specialist must be familiar with the collection, this takes time and a request for reconsideration may occur before the specialist has scrutinized the entire collection. If the committee agrees that the item should be withdrawn, it is appropriate to do so. However, most items requested for reconsideration will be defensible and the committee will back this decision.

Occasionally, the patron will not agree with the committee's recommendation and will wish to pursue the matter further. The principal at this point refers the matter to the superintendent's office with documents confirming school efforts to resolve the matter. Copies of the written request and checklist are submitted to the superintendent's office.

6. A district-level committee, including the library media supervisor(s) (or other appropriate designee), a board of education representative, the library media specialist from the local school, and others as are appropriate within the district, review the item following the process described in steps 3 through 5. Written comments, recommendations, and signatures are appended to the original checklist at the conclusion of this panel's deliberations. The request for reconsideration, the checklist, the school recommendation, and the district committee recommendation are presented to the superintendent whose office informs the patron of the decision.

7. The final decision in the district rests with the board of education or authorized governing body. If the patron is not satisfied with the recommendation made by the district-level committee, an appeal can be made to this council. Its decision is binding within the district and stands unless challenged through the legal system.

Censorship attempts are a reality. The Office for Intellectual Freedom of the American Library Association reported approximately 1,000 attempts in 1982. This number did not include requests for reconsideration that were handled successfully in a low-key manner within the system. A 1980 study conducted by the American Library Association, the Association of American Publishers, and the Association for Supervision and Curriculum Development reported that 26 percent of those responding to a questionnaire had items challenged during the two previous years.[10] When both policy and procedure are in place, the trauma created by a request for reconsideration is reduced.

Equipment Selection

Selecting equipment appropriately is an important consideration for the library media specialist. These purchases are often expensive and selection will affect utilization for years to come. A filmstrip can be weeded fairly painlessly when it no longer fills a need, but a filmstrip projector cannot be casually discarded. Equipment selection, therefore, must be well thought out and planned.

Equipment is merely the vehicle for use of audiovisual materials. It is not purchased as an end in itself, but because it permits specific materials to be integrated into the curriculum. The most important criterion for selection must be that there are materials available that will enhance the curriculum and that they can be purchased provided the appropriate equipment is available.

The computer revolution hit most schools unexpectedly. Suddenly parents and others in the community were demanding that children have access to this new technology. Some schools did not think through the purpose for which these computers would be used and hurried to purchase one or several. Suddenly, teachers realized that there was little educational software for the computers sitting in their schools. These are the computers that can now be found unused in closets. Other schools moved more slowly and developed a plan that included the matching of software to curriculum objectives and provided teacher in-service training. Computer hardware was then purchased to meet the identified needs and the software available. In these schools, the computer has become another tool that addresses the learning styles and needs of children. It is as fully integrated into the teaching process as print materials, films, or pictures.

Teacher acceptance of any new technology is critical before making large scale equipment purchases. Any new technology should be introduced slowly to give teachers both an opportunity to incorporate it into their curriculum and time to get excited about the possibilities it offers.

One teaching technique that failed dismally in the 1960s was the teaching machine. Hailed as a revolution in teaching, this equipment spread like wildfire through school systems. Teacher resistance and insufficient software ultimately caused districts to reconsider its value and today it is difficult to find a classroom with a teaching machine. The technology could have made a difference in teaching methodology; teachers' reluctance invalidated it as a tool.

Videotape, however, has been well accepted by teachers as a means for teaching concepts and enriching understanding. This is due in part to the saturation level of television in our society. What began more than twenty years ago as an esoteric technology is now an accepted vehicle for the instructional program.

The role of the library media specialist in implementing new technology is to help teachers become aware of its value, teach them how to use it, and provide materials that exploit its capabilities. These three steps are crucial if new equipment is to be used and accepted in the classroom.

Increases in the number of equipment items as well as replacement of equipment should be based on need. Equipment should never be purchased without the ability to purchase materials; therefore, any new equipment must simultaneously have a materials source.

Summary

Selection activities fundamentally influence the effectiveness of the library media center. They must occur within the context of a written policy if selection is to meet the needs of the students and teachers. Before writing policy, the specialist must be aware of curriculum needs, library media philosophy, district policy, community values, ages of students, materials formats, and budgets.

The six parts of a selection policy include (1) criteria for selection, (2) selection aids, (3) recommendations, (4) donations, (5) selection responsibility, and (6) reconsideration of materials.

Selection procedures put policy into practice. To actually choose those materials that best meet needs, the specialist must be familiar with the resources currently in the collection and have a plan for development. A variety of sources provide information for selection. These include personal previews, authoritative reviews, and recommended lists of basic collections. Periodicals are purchased to meet the research and recreational needs of students. Titles to be used for research should be chosen in conjunction with the index used.

The initial screening of materials considered for selection is an ongoing process. To organize the collected data, some priority of selection should be imposed, using either computerized or card files.

Requests for reconsideration of materials should follow a specific process with those from an individual being handled at the school level and those from a group or organization being handled at the district level.

Equipment selection is based on identified need and availability of materials. New technologies should be understood and a need created prior to purchase. Quality of any equipment being considered for purchase should be determined.

CHAPTER 7

Budgets and Orders

The responsibilities of a library media specialist include handling the financial transactions of the library media center. This involves working with comparatively large budgets, purchasing wisely, and being fiscally accountable for expenditures. Within a school, in most cases, only the principal has a larger budget; most teachers have little if any budget control and are rarely responsible for requisitions and purchase orders.

This chapter will discuss two primary types of budget allocations, additional revenue sources that may be tapped, and preparation of orders for purchase.

Budgets

Access to financial resources to purchase books, periodicals, audiovisual materials, audiovisual equipment, supplemental print materials, and supplies is essential to the operation of a library media center. Funding for these items must be an ongoing commitment for even the best collection will become dated and inadequate if new items are not purchased regularly.

Library media center budgets are allocated by two methods: a specific dollar amount may be designated at the district or school level for library media expenditures, or the specialist may be required to submit a line item proposal requesting funding.

District Allocation

Districts following a process that allocates funds impartially for all schools are concerned with equity. The governing body wants assurance that all schools at the same level are given resources in a fair, unbiased way. Someone at the district level, with or without recommendations from library media specialists, decides what funds will be meted out for library expenditures. This may be done with an across-the-board figure with each school at the same level receiving an equal amount or, more commonly, on a dollars-per-pupil basis.

The resulting budgets may reflect line item expenditures or a single sum to be apportioned by the school library media specialist. Categorical line items appear as separate budgets for books, periodicals, audiovisual materials, audiovisual equipment, supplies, and so forth. This type of budgeting limits flexibility to purchase according to need, but assures that one category will not consume all the available resources.

A variation of the line item budget combines all print and nonprint materials into a single category while retaining equipment, supplies, audiovisual repair, and so on as separate items.

In some districts, all budgets are combined to give the library media specialist a single operating budget. When this occurs, the library media specialist must follow the same process used in budget building to decide how funds will be spent.

Top-down budgets allocated by someone with higher authority save time as the library media specialist is not required to spend hours planning and writing a budget proposal. In addition, the specialist can gauge fairly accurately what next year's budget will be. Increases are often calculated on a percentage basis and, unless district revenues decrease, are seldom reduced.

When the district allocates sufficient funds based on information from the supervisor or other knowledgeable library media professional, this method of budget dispersal functions satisfactorily. One problem with equity funding is that it does not take into account special needs. Regardless of collection needs, specific dollar amounts are assigned for categorical purchases and the specialist must work within these figures. Another problem is that small schools may not generate large enough budgets to maintain adequate resources.

Budget Proposal

Budget proposals are submitted either at the school level or the district level. When school-based management functions in a district, the principal is allocated a budget that must meet all needs within the school. This may or may not include salaries, but does include textbooks, physical education equipment, furniture, and so forth. Library media expenditures are one part of this overall budget and the specialist must submit a proposal and justify the requested allocation.

Specialists preparing line item budget requests must first gain the support of the principal. This is true whether the school or the district grants the budget. The principal's backing gives validity to the request in the eyes of the district administrators and, of course, at the school level, it is the principal who will accept the proposal and fund it.

The specialist preparing a line item proposal begins by looking at the previous year's budget for a baseline. The specialist determines whether that budget was in line with increased costs and whether it was sufficient to keep the collection and equipment in top condition. Current needs are assessed and the specialist decides if they can be met by a budget in line with the previous one. A history of adequate funding suggests that, unless an extraordinary need has been identified, increases based on inflation factors will be satisfactory.

Too often, the specialist is aware that funding has not kept pace with need. Nationally, book budgets in dollars have increased almost every year (see figure 12), but their purchasing value has not substantially increased. The current book budget in the average library media center buys one-half book per student, a far cry from the two books per student recognized as a standard for keeping book collections at a viable level.[1]

When a given dollar amount has been identified as the figure to be requested in the budget proposal, a narrative providing justification is written to accompany the budget request. This narrative relates expenditures to philosophy and curriculum, looks at long-term goals, and identifies current building-level needs. It can identify who will benefit from any increased expenditure as well as outline the potential risks if the requested funding is not received. If budget allocations for library media items were inadequate in previous years, it may be helpful to compare the current budget to other local schools or to state and national norms.

	Book	Audiovisual
1954	$ .79	$ .15
1959	$1.60	—
1961	$1.47	$ .25
1963	$2.28	—
1974	$4.22	—
1978	$4.25	$1.69
1983	$4.58	$1.79

Source: Eliza T. Dresang, "Lean Years and Fat Years: The Lessons to Be Learned," *The Bowker Annual of Library and Book Trade Information*, 29th ed. (New York: R. R. Bowker Co., 1984): 71.

Figure 12. Average book and audiovisual expenditures per student: 1954–1983

Line item budget proposals are advantageous in that they originate where the resulting funds will be spent. When the specialist carefully prepares such requests, the result is a budget more appropriate to identified needs. A positive library media climate within the school generates the support necessary for funding the proposed budget.

Proposal writing may not be the final step in the budget allocation process, especially if the school or district budgets are inadequate to meet all identified needs within the school. The specialist may be asked to meet with the principal or budget committee to discuss the proposal. The specialist must be armed with facts and be prepared to identify which purchases are essential, which are needed, and which are nice to have but not basic. It must be recognized that the final allocation may fall short of the proposal. The specialist must be realistic in writing a budget proposal, but should not be timid in making those in power aware of library media needs.

When library media support in a school or district is expressed positively through adequate funding, budget proposal writing is the preferred method. Problems arise when library media needs are ranked as a low priority year after year and the funding allocated is insufficient to maintain viable collections. Inequities may result with one school in the district having a model collection while another suffers from inadequate resources. The library media specialist's skill in preparing and defending the budget proposal are the key factors.

Other Revenue Sources

Budgets, as mentioned previously, do not always meet all the identified needs of the library media center. When this occurs, other funding must be found to help meet the deficit. Typical sources include grants, parent/teacher organizations, book fairs, fund-raisers, and lost materials charges and fines. District policy must support these activities. The library media specialist should check the district's policy manual and should elicit approval from the principal before planning a supplemental activity.

Grants. Grants offer the greatest possibility for obtaining large sums of money and are available for almost every conceivable project. Discovering sources of these grants may be difficult, but some are more visible than others.

Currently, districts receive ECIA Chapter 2 funds from the federal government. Some districts allocate a portion of that funding for projects and needs that cannot be fully funded with district revenues. The availability of these funds is relatively easy to ascertain and proposal writing is minimal.

State education agencies may have funds available for specially designated needs, such as library media center innovations, or undesignated funds for validated needs. Proposal writing is required and usually must adhere to specific guidelines.

Numerous grants are available from private foundations and agencies. A library media specialist who wishes to "play the grant game" will need to search the literature diligently, learn the techniques of proposal writing, and discover how to align the needs of the library media center to the criteria specified by the grant.

Few granting agencies will consider requests for merely adding more books or more equipment to the library media center. An innovative approach with identifiable goals and objectives is essential. Some districts and most state education agencies have specialists in grant writing. These people can serve as a valuable resource as they know the successful language and format of grant proposals. Many universities offer graduate courses and seminars in grant writing and these, too, provide the basic skills necessary to successfully seek out and win grants.

Parent/teacher organizations. The local PTA or similar community support group in a school often is actively seeking ways to enrich the educational environment. The library media specialist who presents a plan for using PTA funds to provide better resources for students has a good chance of receiving such funds. Presentations requesting funds from the PTA should focus on benefits to students and should be positively oriented to educational outcomes. Support from the PTA preferably should be in the form of a check to be spent for materials designated by the library media specialist. If the PTA prefers to donate materials, they should be selected from a list prepared by the specialist. PTA awareness of the selection policy and its provision for gift materials will lessen problems in this area.

Book fairs. Book fairs have become a recognized source of funding for many school library media centers. They serve two purposes—generating supplemental funds for the library media center and getting good books into the hands of students. Specialists planning a book fair must first select a sponsor or source that will provide books. This is an important consideration as some book fair vendors have a better quality of titles and bindings than others. The paperwork involved, arrangements for shipping and handling, price discounts, bonuses, and profit margin all enter into the decision-making process. Other specialists who have held book fairs can often clarify these points and give advice on reputable sources that they have used successfully.

The date(s) when the book fair is held affects total sales. Parents at the elementary and junior high levels, where most fairs occur, are the key to success. Students will buy approximately the same number of books regardless of when the fair occurs. Parents constitute an extended market potential and have greater buying power. Days when parents are going to be in the school for conferences, school programs, or other well-attended events are excellent. A preholiday fair in November or early December provides a built-in impetus for holiday gift buying.

Advertising is essential to generate excitement for the fair. Book talks on selected titles that will be available make students aware of books they may want to buy. Discussions of book characters and book reviews by students create extended interest. Communication to the home is essential for making parents aware of the event and for building positive public relations. Fliers, articles in school newsletters, and student-written letters to parents all convey the important information. In-school posters and displays stimulate expectations and anticipation.

A book fair is a time-consuming but legitimate use of library media time. This may be the only opportunity some students have to browse through piles of alluring, new books. The thrill of buying a brand-new book may convert a student into an avid reader and, for all students, the experience is part of the bigger world of books and reading. Therefore, the specialist can feel confident that the fair is a valuable event for students.

Other fund-raisers. Book fairs relate directly to library media activities, but there are a myriad of indirect fund-raising activities that can also generate dollars. Some commercial fund-raisers require the up-front purchase of an item that the school is then allowed to resell at any price it deems appropriate. Library media funds should not be diverted from legitimate purchases of library media materials to purchase fund-raiser items that may or may not sell. Any up-front money should be generated from the principal's office, a parent/teacher organization, or so forth. The library media specialist should select a reputable source for the fund-raiser that permits return of and reimbursement for all unsold items. Purchase on consignment is the better approach.

Some fund-raisers, such as bake sales, are based on donated goods. The attitude of patrons toward such fund-raisers and the required coordination time should be carefully considered before undertaking such an event.

Any fund-raiser's success will depend on advertising of the event and communication to the home. It is essential that the principal be consulted before investigating fund-raising activities and that reports be given regularly.

Lost materials charges and fines. Most schools charge students for lost or irreparably damaged materials. The money collected is used to buy replacement items, either the exact title or something more recent but in the same subject area.

When a fee is paid for a lost item, the specialist pulls the shelflist card and puts it in a file marked "lost items." When using a computerized system, the specialist enters the appropriate data into the computer where it can be retrieved when needed or keeps the print-out information on lost items in a notebook or file.

The item is not replaced immediately for two reasons. First, the student may locate the item and return it. If the item has been replaced, this will result in duplication where possibly it is not needed. Second, it is inefficient to purchase a single item at a time. Most specialists accumulate these funds during the school year and spend them either in the spring to close out the accounting process or in the fall after items returned over the summer are reintegrated into the collection.

Fines, when charged, are a minimal additional source of income. Although this is not the primary purpose of fines, money is generated and can be used as designated by policy. Many specialists purchase posters, supplies, and other miscellaneous items with fine money.

All of the additional revenue sources discussed supplement a primary budget: they cannot supplant it. When any of these funding resources is sought, the specialist is committing time and effort that must be balanced against the potential value of the revenue and the loss of time for interactions with students and teachers.

Ordering

Once the budget is in place, the items selected are matched to the budget allocation, a purchase source is decided on, and additional related decisions are made that result in a requisition or purchase order being generated. Although the process follows the same steps regardless of what is being purchased, there are varying considerations for books, periodicals, audiovisual materials, and equipment.

Books

Budget Alignment

Determining the number of titles that can be purchased using the budget allocation is a function of selection. However, deciding how much of the budget will be allocated at any given time of the year is part of the budgeting process. District operating procedures may recommend equitable distribution of purchase commitment by month or by quarter, or they may place greater emphasis on disbursement schedules.

Purchase Source

Many districts have a central facility that handles all aspects of purchasing after the selection process has taken place in the school. In these districts, the specialist submits the selection list (with a purchase requisition if needed) and awaits the arrival of fully processed books. Other specialists do not have this luxury and must decide which source is most qualified to fill the order. Most commonly a jobber, such as Baker and Taylor, Follett, or Ingram is chosen to handle a large book order.

There are several advantages to using a jobber to fill the order rather than going directly to publishers. First is the considerable saving in paperwork: a single order form, such as that reproduced in figure 13, is sufficient. A second consideration is that a jobber has a large inventory of books and offers discounts on publishers' list prices, resulting in more books for the money.

If the school system does not identify a specific jobber to whom orders must be routed, the specialist should explore the options available and select a jobber whose purchasing procedures and dependability meet her or his needs. Speed in receiving the total order, number of out of stock items, quality, and accuracy are factors to consider when deciding which jobber(s) to use.

Not all book orders can be processed through a primary jobber. Occasionally, school library media specialists find it necessary to order directly from the publisher.

A third source for purchasing books is a local bookstore. This procedure is appropriate when need for a specific title is immediate or when small amounts remain in the budget that must be expended before the end of the budget period.

Bindings

In addition to author, title, publisher, and price, it may be necessary to specify the type of binding desired. There are five bindings generally used in books with trade bindings being the most common. Unless the specialist requests a specific binding, the trade binding is usually sent. It is important, therefore, to recognize the different types of bindings and to know when each is most appropriate.

Paperback. A paperback book, in general, is smaller in size than the hardcover book of the same title and is bound with paper covers on the outside. The pages are made of inexpensive paper and are glued to the spine. Paperbacks are less expensive to buy but do not survive numerous circulations. Paperbacks provide a good way to add copies of titles that will have short-term popularity or that may entice reluctant readers. Paperbacks should be purchased as a supplement to hardcover books and should not be purchased as a primary collection.

Prebind. Prebound books are the sturdiest and longest lasting of all the bindings and also the most expensive. Children's titles can be ordered as prebinds and some compa-

Instructions

1. Double space.
2. Must be in alphabetical order by either author or title.

Vendor

Name: _____

Address: _____

Date _____ Order No. _____

Address: _____

L. M. Specialist: _____

Copies	Author	Title	Publisher	Price	Special Instructions

Figure 13. Book order form

nies, such as Bound-To-Stay-Bound, specialize in this type of binding. Prebound books have good quality buckram for the outside cover, are side sewn, and have a strong hinge and reinforced corners. The cover often has an illustration imprinted on it. Prebound books are perfect for picture books and the most popular children's literature titles. Prebound books are very stiff when new, but this disadvantage quickly disappears and their long life through many circulations becomes an advantage. Expensive prebinds should be purchased only for titles that will have extensive use.

Publisher library binding. Books with publisher library bindings are sturdier than trade volumes and are purchased primarily for school and public libraries. The outside cover of a PLB should be plastic-impregnated cloth and the book should have a side-sewn signature, linen-reinforced hinge, and double-fold corners. This type of binding is ideal for books expected to have heavy circulation at the secondary level and for many books not purchased as prebinds at the elementary level.

Reinforced paperback. Paperback books are given increased circulation life when purchased with a reinforced binding. The paper covers are replaced with hard covers of plastic-coated board, and a longer-lasting glue is used. Companies such as Demco and American Econoclad specialize in reinforced paperbacks. Books with this binding fill the need for multiple-use copies that will be circulated over a long period of time: classics are a prime example.

Trade. Trade bindings are those found on books at the local bookstore. They are the most common binding and the one normally supplied unless the specialist requests otherwise. The outside cover is generally made of cloth-covered boards, and center-sewn signatures hold the pages together. There is no special reinforcement at the spine, hinge, or corners. Trade editions serve adequately for materials that will not circulate extensively. These bindings normally are ordered for nonfiction titles where extensive use is not anticipated.

Cataloging

The final decision to be made before books are ordered is who will do the cataloging. In districts where cataloging is done centrally, all materials are shelf-ready when they are received at the school. For specialists who do not have this service, cataloging must either be purchased from the supplier or handled on-site.

Local school cataloging is now much easier to do thanks to Cataloging In Publication (CIP). Almost all books purchased for school library media centers have cataloging information printed on the verso of the title page. The greatest disadvantage of local school cataloging is the time involved. To be cost effective there must be clerical staff trained to prepare cards or to enter the appropriate data into the computer. This creates a lag between the time when materials are received in the school and when they are shelf-ready. The advantage to local cataloging is that there is total control over call numbers and unique situations can be accommodated. However, unless support staff has abundant time and skills, the disadvantages of on-site cataloging far outweigh the advantages.

Complete processing for books can be purchased for a nominal fee (70 cents to $1.56 in 1980)[2] from most jobbers. The school specialist or the district supervisor submits cataloging criteria that conform to the existing collections. Books arrive with catalog cards, check-out card and pocket, and mylar jacket. Final processing can be handled quickly in the school. As more library media centers become computerized, more jobbers are offering cataloging data on disks that can easily be loaded into the local computer system.

Availability Cycles

Publishers tend to have the greatest number of titles available early in the calendar year. This is because federal taxes are levied on books remaining in warehouses at the end of the year. Hence, more books are published during late winter to early spring. Specialists should be aware that late fall orders may show an increase in out-of-stock items.

Remainder wholesalers have a corresponding increase in titles at the end of the calendar year as they buy excess stock directly from the publishers. In buying from these sources, the specialist must be careful to select quality materials as some remainders are books that did not receive good reviews and, hence, did not sell at regular prices. Remainders tend to have trade bindings, a fact that must also be considered.

Jobbers maintain a year-round stock of books as they sell to public libraries as well as to school library media centers. However, recognizing that schools order primarily in the spring and fall, their stock of school titles is highest at these times.

Discounts

Some jobbers offer discounts based on total school or district purchases. Others sell books at the same price to bookstores, public libraries, and school library media centers regardless of volume from any single buyer. Still others offer discounts for payment received within a 30- or 60-day period. Specialists should be aware that not all books are discounted at the same rate. The binding selected may determine the discount with prebinds having a minimal discount and trade editions the greatest.

Requisitions and Purchase Orders

Schools have varying processes for ordering materials and library media specialists must follow designated procedures. Generally, this involves filling out a requisition form stating vendor name and address, what is being purchased, and the amount of the order.

Book orders can seldom be calculated to an exact amount because of discounts and out-of-print or out-of-stock cancellations. If a jobber is used, a "Do Not Exceed" figure allows the jobber to fill the order up to the specified dollar amount. A first-choice list and a supplemental list with a total exceeding the purchase price by 20 percent to 30 percent takes into account those titles that are not available. It should be stated on the order form that substitution of titles not on the list is unacceptable.

The book list, in alphabetical order by author or title, is attached to the requisition or purchase order. A copy is made for use as a checklist in the accounting process when materials are received.

The requisition with the attached book list is then signed by the principal and sent to the district purchasing department for preparation of a purchase order. If purchase orders originate at the school, this intermediary step is omitted. Whoever has budget authority, however, must clear the requisition or purchase order and verify that funds exist to cover the expenditure.

Audiovisual Materials

Budget Alignment

Audiovisual materials are prioritized in the same way as books with purchases confined to the parameters of the budget. These items vary greatly in price; for example, an audio cassette tape may cost only $10 while a large model or kit may cost $250 or more. The amount of use an item will receive, the alternative of borrowing the item from a central media center, and the need for the item should be taken into account when aligning selection and budget.

Purchase Source

Audiovisual materials are purchased directly from a distributor or a representative who handles several companies. To date, there is no clearinghouse for audiovisual materials that includes all distributors' holdings as jobbers do for books although this may be an option in the future.

Special Offers

Some audiovisual companies regularly have special offers intended to encourage purchase of their materials. These offers may be price discounts or, more often, free materials or equipment if an order totals a specified amount. If the minimum dollar amount required to qualify for the bonus exceeds the amount the specialist intends to spend, orders may be batched with those of another school and the bonus materials or discount shared. Many companies will cooperate with this type of transaction.

Archival Copies

Computer programs, audio cassettes, and records need back-up copies in case damage occurs to the original. Copyright law permits an archival copy that is not used as part of the circulating collection. Many computer disks are programmed so that the buyer cannot duplicate the disk. Locking the program prevents unauthorized duplication, but also negates the possibility of holding an archival copy. Purchase orders for computer programs should specify that an archival back-up be included.

Cataloging

Many audiovisual distributors include catalog cards with their products either at no charge or for a minimal fee. These cards usually use Dewey decimal numbers and may not fit the library media center's format. However, even when computerized cataloging is used or when the format is incompatible with that of the center, the purchased card sets provide all the information needed and save time for the cataloger.

Shipping and Handling

Many audiovisual distributors charge for shipping and handling orders. This additional sum, either a percentage or specified amount, must be taken into account when preparing orders. The company's catalog should provide this information.

Requisitions and Purchase Orders

Each order to a distributor requires a separate requisition or purchase order. Complete descriptive information should be given including title, type of material, number of parts (2 filmstrips, 2 cassette tapes), catalog number, and price. The amount designated for shipping and handling should be stipulated as should any special instructions and reference to bonuses or discounts.

Periodicals

Budget Alignment

Thousands of periodicals and journals roll off printing presses each week. Fortunately, not all titles are suitable for school library media centers. Selection criteria and procedures apply to the purchase of periodicals and must be considered along with budget constraints when purchasing these items for the school library media center.

The titles selected, as described in the previous chapter, must be prioritized to meet the budget. Where budgets are small, this is a Herculean task. The funds available are matched to those titles most suitable for the intended users. Unfortunately, it is almost impossible to calculate the exact cost of a periodical order. Discounts, price increases, and unavailable titles cannot be fully known in advance.

Purchase Source

It is possible, of course, to order periodicals directly from the publisher. Indeed, some, such as local newspapers, must be ordered this way. Most periodicals, however, are best ordered through a periodical service center, such as EBSCO or Turner Subscription Agency. There are several advantages to using a subscription service. The paperwork is reduced as only one requisition or purchase order is generated and, after the first year, the only changes to a standing order are deletions and additions. All subscriptions can be arranged to begin in the same month (usually September), eliminating the constant battle to keep subscription orders current. When problems arise, and they do frequently, the service is notified and it rectifies the situation. The subscription service has direct contact with the periodical clearinghouse while an individual specialist may be frustrated by corresponding with numerous publishers.

No service can make periodical ordering painless. The more subscriptions ordered, the more frequently problems surface. In addition to solving problems of missing or late issues, canceled titles, wrong number of copies, and so on, a subscription service eliminates the difficulty of maintaining separate renewals with individual magazine publishers.

Discounts

Discounts are a fact of life when ordering periodicals. They are available directly from the publisher or from a subscription service. Publisher discounts are primarily come-ons to induce the subscriber to try the magazine. The price rarely holds for renewals, but the initial subscription may be half-price or less. Periodical services, on the other hand, give across-the-board discounts year after year and may honor publisher discounts as well.

Changing Market

Periodicals are published to respond to every imaginable interest. Publication begins as people become fascinated with a new topic and ceases as interest wanes and costs exceed revenues. Giants in one era will vanish in the next; hence the demise of *Life* and *Look*. Children's magazines respond to changing times as well and, although the old standbys such as *Children's Activities* and *Jack and Jill* have survived over the years, others have come and gone. The alert library media specialist must monitor each periodical selection for both currency and interest to readers.

Requisitions and Purchase Orders

Subscriptions sent directly to the publisher must be accompanied by individual requisitions or purchase orders. Requisitions or purchase orders prepared for a periodical service are attached to the list of titles desired. The total cost stated on the requisition or purchase order reflects discounts and allows for price increases and so is not an exact cost, but an educated estimate.

Regardless of the source, the requisition or purchase order must contain certain information.

1. Start-up month
2. Number of years to be billed (Multiyear orders are frequently discounted more than single-year orders, but multiyear budget commitments may be against local operating policy.)
3. Subscriber name and address for delivery
4. Indication if subscription runs nine months only (Some periodicals may be purchased for nine months with school orders. This may save money, but may leave a gap in back issues.)

Audiovisual Equipment

Budget Alignment

Equipment needs must be aligned to the budget somewhat differently than other purchases. A savings in initial cost on a piece of equipment may not be a bargain over a period of years. Quality and performance take precedence over price. As mentioned earlier, equipment purchases are based on the audiovisual materials available for use. When ordering computers, the specialist designates those compatible with the available software. When videotape players are needed, the choice of VHS or Beta will depend on the format of tapes available.

Industrial Models versus Consumer Models

Equipment is often available in two different qualities—industrial and consumer. Equipment intended for industrial use is built for durability, to withstand repeated heavy use by a variety of operators and to remain intact when moved frequently. With this durability comes an increased price. Equipment intended for consumers' home use is built for the less demanding environment of family life, meaning it is anticipated that fewer individuals will operate the equipment, it will be moved less frequently, and it will not run constantly day after day. It is not always necessary to order industrial-quality audiovisual equipment, but it is important that the specialist understands the two designations and orders appropriately.

Requisitions and Bidding

This step implies that a central purchasing department will solicit bids and prepare the final purchase order. In preparing a requisition, therefore, the specialist describes as exactly as possible the features and qualities that the machine must have. Some districts will accept brand names and model numbers and will get bids on that item only. Some will accept brand names and models to use as a basis for bids, but will not limit bids to the specific brand. Others permit only a description of the item, which is used for bidding. The specialist must be cognizant of district practice. The requisition requires an estimated cost and a list or advertised price will usually suffice. The requisition is completed at the school level, appropriate signatures are obtained, and it is then forwarded to the purchasing department.

The purchasing department prepares a specifications list for bid. Requisitions may be batched to make up larger orders that can elicit lower bids. If the district has a timetable for bidding at designated times of the year, the library media specialist should be aware of this and submit requisitions accordingly. The district may bid on a yearly basis for frequently purchased items. In this instance, the specialist can call the district's purchasing department, get an exact quote on cost, and submit the requisition at any time during the year. After bids have been returned by vendors, purchase orders are generated and filled.

Purchase Orders

Purchase orders are usually generated in a school when there is no central clearinghouse. Although bidding is not practical for purchasing one or two pieces of equipment, the library media specialist should check with local dealers to determine which one will provide the item at the best price. The specialist should decide on the brand and model before contacting dealers for price.

District or school procedures may dictate when orders must be submitted. When procedure permits the library media specialist to order materials at any time during the year, a large order in the spring or early fall will ensure that books, audiovisual materials, and equipment are received in time to be used during the entire school year. Initial orders for library media items may not expend the entire budget allocation; by saving a portion of the budget, needs that arise during the school year can be met. Two or at most three orders per year are a guideline that should be maintained. School library media centers cannot get bogged down trying to account for multiple orders to the same source and, most important, what is ordered in January may not be used until the following September. Careful planning with teachers will enable the specialist to order effectively so that materials are on hand when they are needed.

It is almost impossible to be 100 percent accurate in allocating funds when ordering books, periodicals, audiovisual materials, and equipment. The library media specialist, therefore, must keep account control records of expenditures in order to zero out budgets as nearly as possible. Some districts zero out all library media accounts at year's end with any balances going back into the general education fund; others permit carryover sums. Regardless of district procedures, it is not wise to leave large balances as this indicates poor management practice.

Total expenditure of the budget is an important aspect of budget building. It is difficult to justify increased or even status quo funding when significant balances remain from the previous year's budget. Overspending does not win supporters either. Account control will be discussed in detail in the next chapter.

Summary

School library media funds may be budgeted categorically by the district or by the library media specialist's preparation of a line item request proposal. Additional funding may be generated through grants, parent/teacher organizations, book fairs, fund-raisers, lost materials fees, and fines. Book orders must be aligned to budget and a purchase source selected if the district does not have a standard procedure. Ordering directly from a publisher or through a jobber are the two primary options with local bookstore purchases filling a supplemental need.

The five book bindings primarily purchased for school use are paperback, prebound, publisher library binding, reinforced paperback, and trade. Cataloging may be done on-site or by a central facility, or it may be purchased through the jobber or publisher. Availability, remainders, and discounts are considered before preparing a requisition or purchase order. Audiovisual materials are usually purchased through the distributor. Special offers, archival copies, cataloging, and shipping and handling charges are considered and a requisition or purchase order generated. Periodicals are generally purchased through a periodical service with consideration given to discounts and the changing market. Requisitions and purchase orders detail specifications. Audiovisual equipment orders are based on intended use and bids are the recognized method for obtaining the lowest price.

CHAPTER 8

Budget Accounting
and Materials Processing

Materials selection and ordering are administrative functions of collection development. They set the stage for the next steps in the process. Expenditures must be accounted for and budgets monitored. As items are received in the library media center, they must be processed and made available to users quickly. This chapter will guide the library media specialist in setting up and maintaining account control procedures, tracking items ordered, accounting for materials when they are received, and processing items for use.

These are ongoing procedures as items ordered will arrive at various times. Large spring orders may be delivered during the summer with the bulk of an order accounted for by September. However, even specialists who order primarily once a year will find it rare that accounts can be closed at the beginning of the school year. When ordering occurs throughout the year, as is preferred to meet changing educational needs, the paper flow is continuous.

Establishing Account Control Procedures

Creating a System

Purchasing items creates a prodigious amount of paperwork that must be organized to facilitate management. The first document that must be considered is the one that notifies the library media specialist of the budget amount and account number(s) to be used during the current fiscal year.

Whether a single sum is used for all items or separate accounts are kept for books, periodicals, audiovisual materials, equipment, and supplies, the specialist originates documentation for each category.

Paper

When only a paper trail exists, establish individual manila file folders for each purchase area. These folders can be used to track all expenditures as well as hold all related paperwork. Next, set up account control sheets. These sheets, illustrated in figure 14, provide space to record all transactions that occur within the designated budget. The budget account number, descriptive name, and budget amount are filled in as soon as the library media specialist receives the official budget. The account control sheet is then stapled onto the front cover of the folder. As requisitions are written against that account, the data are recorded on the budget control sheet. A running estimated balance reveals at a glance the amount remaining for additional purchases.

Account Number _____

Budget Amount _____

Vendor	Date Ordered	Req. No.	P. O. No.	Est. Amount	Est. Balance	Date Received	Actual Amount	Actual Balance

Figure 14. Account control sheet

A copy of each complete requisition is filed in the folder. If district forms do not permit the library media specialist to retain a copy of the requisition, a photocopy should be kept. This copy is filed in numerical order by requisition number or alphabetically by company or vendor name. Alphabetical order is preferred as the vendor's name is apparent on shipments while the requisition or purchase order numbers may be more difficult to find. Any attachments, such as lists of books or periodicals, are stapled behind the original requisition. When copies of purchase orders are received, they are checked to verify that requisition and purchase order amounts agree. The purchase order is then stapled on top of the requisition and returned to the folder.

A variation of this system uses a three-ring binder with tabbed dividers identifying the purchase areas. A master account control sheet placed at the front of the binder can monitor the activity of all accounts with individual account activity being recorded on separate account control sheets placed behind the appropriate tab. As in the folder system, the purchase requisition, purchase order, lists of titles, and other attachments should be stapled together before being placed in the binder. Budget transactions continue to be accounted for on the account control sheets.

Computer

A computer simplifies the account tracking process. A spreadsheet is set up with separate headings for each account and its budgeted allocation. The advantage of the spreadsheet is that columns can be added or deleted, amounts changed, and new totals calculated without having to alter previously entered data.[1] If floppy disks are used, the specialist labels one specifically for budget purposes.

As requisitions are written, the information is entered into the computer, which automatically calculates balances. Purchase order numbers are added as received and the account information is accessed or printed as desired.

File folders are maintained for the paper copies of requisitions and purchase orders and for the printed lists of books and periodicals appended to the orders. There is no benefit to saving title lists in the computer as the specialist will need to work from the hard copy as materials are received.

Tracking Orders

When requisitions are generated at the school level, a district office prepares the purchase orders. This may take days or weeks depending on the efficiency and work load of that department. The specialist must be aware that orders will not get to the vendor until the purchase order has been generated. The delay time may be long if orders on an anticipated budget are submitted in the spring, before summer vacation. These orders may remain in the district office until the beginning of the new fiscal year (July 1, August 1, or September 1) before they are sent to suppliers. A copy of the purchase order sent to the library media center will alert the specialist to the date when it was created.

Purchase orders are reconciled with requisitions when the specialist receives them. Minor differences in total cost are not significant, but large variations require follow-up to verify the reason for the discrepancy. It is necessary to compare titles, item specifications, and item numbers (where applicable) to confirm that the order sent to the vendor is the same as the one requisitioned by the library media specialist. Transposition of numbers can mean that a wrong item will be sent. Any problems should be discussed with the responsible personnel and corrective action taken.

After purchase orders are written, there is a realistic time lag until the items ordered arrive. The specialist must be aware of the normal shipping time periods. If a reasonable time has passed and there has been no contact from the vendor, follow-up procedures are initiated. A call to the sales representative or shipping point, or a letter of inquiry, usually is sufficient to clarify matters and move the process along. To keep on top of this and other problems that arise, the specialist needs to review budget control records and file folders at least once a month.

Change Orders

Change orders are a fact of library media life that cannot be avoided. Because book titles are subject to a variety of cancellations, over-ordering is the usual procedure. Out of print, out of stock, temporarily out of stock, and not yet printed are the most common reasons given by vendors for not shipping individual titles.

Audiovisual materials and periodicals are most subject to price increases. The primary reason for a price increase is that the specialist used an old catalog when ordering. It is also possible, especially when an old catalog is used, that the item ordered is no longer available. Use of up-to-date sources is essential for accurate record keeping. Periodical price increases cannot be predicted. If a negative balance in a budget will precipitate cancellation of an entire order, it is wise for the specialist to leave a small amount in the account to cover any increases.

As changes to purchase orders are received, they are noted in the appropriate place. On the budget control sheet, price increases are recorded by putting a slash through the estimated amount and writing in the revised amount. The date the change was made is noted and the estimated balance is adjusted accordingly. When a computerized spreadsheet is used, the new figures replace the old and the computer calculates the revised balance. The change notice is attached to the purchase order it affects and is retained in the file folder.

Items that are unavailable must be canceled from the list of titles so that the specialist can accurately figure the revised status of the order. This is quickly accomplished with a red pen or pencil notation made in front of the title. Abbreviations, such as O.P. (out of print), T.O.S. (temporarily out of stock), and O.S. (out of stock), speed the process and alert the specialist to titles that may be reordered and those that will not be available. Cancellation of individual titles will not change the total purchase price if extra titles were ordered in anticipation of this problem.

Back Orders

Back orders most often apply to audiovisual materials and equipment. When an item is back ordered, it means that the shipping source cannot send the item immediately, but will do so at a later date. Sometimes this is only a matter of weeks, but occasionally back orders will linger for months. Close monitoring of budget accounts will reveal persistent back orders and alert the specialist to resolve the problem with the supplier.

Approaching deadlines give impetus to the specialist to cancel the back-ordered item and order something guaranteed to be delivered within the necessary time period. Even when deadlines are not a problem, the specialist should contact the supplier about any item that has been back ordered for eight to twelve weeks. Unless the item will be delivered within two to four additional weeks, it should be canceled. Canceled back-ordered items, if especially needed, should be reordered later.

Processing Orders Received

Normally, within a few weeks after a purchase order is generated, the items will be shipped by the vendor. If processing occurs at a centralized district location, books and audiovisual materials will be shipped to that site. The specialist may be notified of their arrival at this point. Materials and equipment delivered directly to the library media center are accounted for more quickly, but the library media center staff must then complete the processing.

No matter when items physically arrive at the school, it is the library media specialist's responsibility to verify that the order has been filled accurately. Mistakes happen and the specialist must correct them immediately.

Packing Verification

When items are delivered to the library media center, the first step is to verify the contents of the carton with the enclosed invoice or packing slip. This is important because billing will be based on this information.

Books are checked to make sure that the author and title listed on the packing slip correspond exactly to those on the book jacket or cover. Titles of audiovisual materials are also checked in this way. Audiovisual equipment is inspected to see that the model number on the packing slip agrees with that on the item and that all parts listed on the slip were packed in the carton. Periodicals are not mailed with a packing slip.

Purchase Order Verification

The next step is to verify that the items received are those that were actually requested. The items are compared with the purchase order or its accompanying list to assure that each is correct. Each component is checked for defects or errors. Again, mistakes do happen and it is much easier to correct a problem at this point than after the item has circulated.

Books are checked first to see that the author and title of the copy received correspond to what was ordered. While the book is being held by the specialist or assistant to verify author and title, it is also checked quickly for errors. Common printing errors include missing pages, pages inserted upside down, pages not fully cut or miscut, the cover upside down, and the spine not imprinted. If a cursory check reveals no obvious faults, a notation that the book has been received is made near the title on the order sheet. The date received is the logical notation as this provides account activity feedback to the specialist during the monthly review of budgets and accounts.

Student helpers can assist with a more thorough checking of books for misbinding as they "ease" the books. This process involves gently sliding one's fingers along the spine edge of the page, working page by page and alternating from front to back until reaching the middle of the book.

Audiovisual materials are checked against the purchase order to verify the title and number of components (if applicable). Most audiovisual materials are guaranteed and the specialist does not need to view or listen to the item to locate defects. Computer programs may have a shorter guarantee period and should be inspected briefly to confirm that the contents will boot and that the title is the same as that ordered. After the item is checked, the date received is marked on the purchase order. The packing slip is then signed and dated.

Periodical records are kept to verify that each issue is received in a reasonable period of time. Tracking forms, such as those from Demco, Brodart, or Highsmith (see figure 15), or a computer spreadsheet may be used. If records are kept on cards, they should be alphabetically arranged in a 3″ × 5″ file box or, when numerous subscriptions are ordered, in special periodical record files.

When a periodical service is the ordering source, a computerized print-out of titles is customarily sent to the library media specialist some time after subscriptions have begun. This print-out should be compared to the list submitted with the purchase order and to the specialist's tracking record. Any discrepancies should be reported immediately. Periodicals normally are paid for in advance. When a subscription title is not received or an issue is missing, an inquiry or claim must be made to correct the situation as soon as possible.

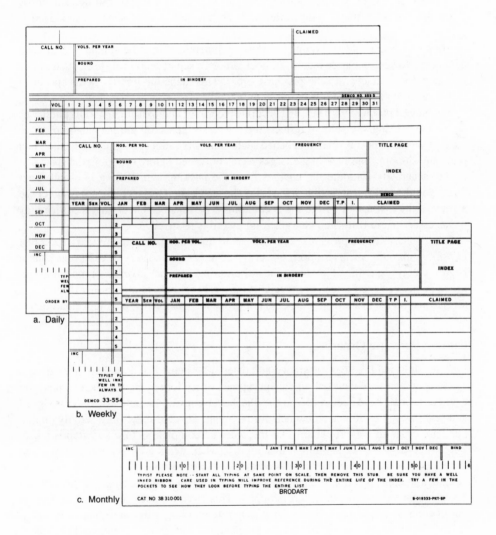

Figure 15. Tracking forms for periodicals received daily, weekly, and monthly

Equipment is immediately inspected for shipping damage. Any obvious damage to the carton should be noted prior to opening and the box should remain as it was delivered and the vendor notified. Even if there is no apparent damage to the carton, if any part appears to have been damaged in the mail, the shipping carton should be saved and the vendor notified.

Audiovisual equipment should be tested immediately to make sure it is operating correctly. Most equipment has only a ninety-day warranty, which makes it vital that the item be verified as fully functional before it is used in the classroom.

Updating Account Control Records

Upon verification that the items received are exactly those that were ordered, expenditures are recorded on the account control sheets. The invoice, or billing, amount is cross-checked with that on the order and the account control sheet is amended if necessary.

Book orders are seldom complete in one shipment and may be spread over several deliveries. To keep accurate records of book orders, a separate control sheet, such as that in figure 16, is attached to the purchase order. This helps the library media specialist know the current status of a book order at any time.

The biggest problem with keeping accurate records of audiovisual materials purchases is that the packing slip seldom reflects the price. The space on the packing slip where the cost should appear is often blackened so the numbers cannot be read. Unless the exact price and shipping and handling charges were confirmed before ordering, the specialist cannot accurately compute the charges from the packing slip. Billing is usually sent directly to the office responsible for writing the checks and the specialist may never see a copy of the invoice. A call to the accounting department to check invoice price may be necessary to confirm final charges if no record is received.

Periodicals, as noted previously, are subject to fluctuations in price. When a specialist is working through a subscription service, price increases and service discounts cannot be accurately determined at the time of ordering. As no invoice or packing slip accompanies each periodical, the specialist must rely on the accounting sheet sent by the service and on feedback from the person or office responsible for paying for purchases.

Closing Purchase Orders

Packing slips and invoices are signed and dated after items listed on them are verified. These documents are then sent to the appropriate office for payment. When all items on a purchase order have been received and checked, a copy of the purchase order is signed and sent through established channels for payment. This closes off any activity on that purchase order so it is important that the order be complete before this step is taken. Purchase orders are not submitted as complete when items are back ordered or when shipment of some part of the order is delayed for any reason.

Dollar amounts on book orders, especially, may not be completely expended after all books requested on the order are shipped. This may be due to a large number of out-of-print or out-of-stock books, or it may reflect a larger discount than was anticipated. The specialist may submit a supplemental list of books to expend the balance remaining on the purchase order. The supplemental list must refer to the purchase order number and include a statement such as "Titles to complete Purchase Order (number)— Do Not Exceed (dollar amount) remaining." These supplemental lists may be sent

Date Received						Invoice or Credit #						$ Amount — Pd. or Cr.					P. O. ____ Balance on P. O.				

Figure 16. Book order control sheet

directly to the vendor unless district policy requires approval from a supervisor. When district processing services exist, a copy of this transaction must be forwarded to that office as well.

District or school procedure may require cancellation of the balance of a purchase order when all items have been received. When this occurs, the specialist should make sure the balance will be refunded to the specific budget rather than to a general fund.

Budget Control

Accurate accounting of budget expenditures is the key to using all available funds. As noted previously, it is not always possible to verify payment amounts from invoices or packing slips. If at all possible, school library media center records should be verified with those at the central office. Some districts provide computer print-outs for this purpose while others have no consistent reporting method.

As budgets are expended and paperwork is completed, the specialist can combine all school copies of purchase orders and account records into one folder for filing. Records are usually kept at the district level as well, but it is advisable to keep copies of expenditures for approximately five years. All extraneous materials should be deleted to prevent files from becoming overburdened. Unless policy or procedure of the school or district dictates otherwise, records should be discarded after seven years maximum. Beyond that period, it is very doubtful whether anyone will ever need to refer to them.

One final caveat of budget control is that the specialist must be aware of all deadlines regarding budgets. There is usually a cutoff date after which requisitions on a specific budget will not be processed. A different date normally is used for clearing all purchase orders. After this date, all orders are canceled.

It is important that the library media specialist know whether carryover funds are permitted. Carryover money is allocated one year, but not encumbered in requisitions or purchase orders before the cutoff date. Some districts add this balance to the next year's budget while others return it to the general fund. Even when carryover funds are permitted, it is best to expend the entire budget during the normal budget year. Excessive carryovers may be interpreted as an excess of funds and may signal a corresponding budget reduction if the specialist has no valid reason for holding some of the money.

Library-generated Revenues

In addition to regular budgets, most library media centers record some student financial transactions. These include fine payments and restitution for lost or damaged materials. No matter how minimal these amounts are, they must be accounted for and records kept.

The student should be given a receipt to verify payment. This may be as simple as marking the student's fine notice paid and initialing and dating it. The money received should be noted in a log indicating date, amount, and source.

What is done with this revenue depends on district policy. The library media specialist may be required to place all income into a bona fide existing account where it can be expended along with district-generated funds. Other districts permit independent school or library media center accounts where the money is deposited into a separate checking account or used for petty cash expenditures. It is vital when a petty cash account is used that expenditures be carefully recorded and that debits and credits balance.

The key purpose of the accounting process is to leave a clear and accurate audit trail that can be verified. This is done for the protection of the library media staff as well as for district records.

Processing New Items

After the account control sheets have been updated, or simultaneously if the specialist has sufficient assistance, new items should be processed and made shelf ready. There is no excuse for new materials remaining unused because they have not been processed. Getting new materials and equipment into the hands of the users as quickly as possible makes sense from curricular, financial, and public relations viewpoints.

Books

District Processing

When books are processed at a centralized location in a district, much of the work of preparing them for the shelves is completed before delivery to the school. District personnel verify that cataloging follows established guidelines and is done correctly. Cards, pockets, book jackets, bar codes, detection strips, and so forth will be in place according to standard procedures. The cataloging may include the accession number (if bar codes are not used). With manual systems, the library media specialist must only separate the shelflist card from the catalog cards, complete the shelf list card if necessary, and file all cards in their appropriate location (see chapter 9). If an automated system is used, the specialist updates the information either by uploading the computer from a disk provided by the district or by initial entering of data from a list or from shelflist cards provided by the district.

The books are placed on the shelves as soon as possible. It is not necessary to file cards in the catalog before making books available to students and teachers. However, if a computerized circulation system is used, the system must be updated before students attempt to check out books.

Purchased Processing

Books purchased from the vendor with complete processing can be made shelf ready in a minimal amount of time. There are a few additional steps to be taken beyond those described under district processing.

It is wise for the specialist to verify that the call numbers assigned by the vendor comply with the cataloging specification submitted. Errors may occur and anomalies within a system create problems, for example, a library media center that shelves biography under the designation *B* will find it difficult to shelve a biography that arrives with the call number 92.

Cards must match the book for which they are intended. To verify accuracy of computerized formats, the specialist should print a hard copy of the information stored on the disk received from the vendor and make sure specifications are correct.

Unless specifically contracted, vendor cataloging does not include security system detection strips and, if these are used, they must be inserted at the school. Most vendors do not assign an accession or copy number; this is done locally. Final processing must be completed at the school.

Original Cataloging

Original cataloging in the school is done by the library media staff. The book is delivered much as it would be found on the shelves of a bookstore. There are no catalog cards, pocket, check-out card, spine identification call number, or mylar cover to protect the jacket and book. The staff completes all processing before shelving the book for circulation.

Not long ago, original cataloging was a time-consuming challenge to library media specialists. After identifying the primary subject of a book, the specialist poured over the Dewey decimal system guides trying to select the most suitable classification number. Specialists with less time to pursue the illusive numbers frequently took a shortcut and used those given in the *Sears List of Subject Headings Catalog.*

Cataloging follows very definite rules detailed in the second edition of *Anglo-American Cataloguing Rules* (*AACR2*). The revised edition of *AACR2* will be more useful in schools with computerized catalogs as it provides a greater level of detail in defining a document and uses punctuation that will be recognized by the computer.

Today, most books purchased for school library media centers have cataloging information on the verso of the title page. Cataloging In Publication (CIP) not only saves time, but also increases consistency. When the specialist was responsible for selecting the Dewey number, it was possible for multiple copies of a title to end up shelved in different locations due to various interpretations of the subject.

Using cataloging information provided, a paraprofessional rather than the library media specialist can catalog a book. Card sets are still individually typed in some centers, but with the advent of memory typewriters and computerized card-making programs, original production of cards can be done much faster and more efficiently. Information is entered in the typewriter or computer one time and all the cards are printed in a matter of seconds. When using a computerized card maker, it is important to get the heaviest card stock that will run through the printer. Flimsy stock will not survive repeated handling in the card catalog.

Catalog card sets may be purchased from a variety of sources, such as the Library of Congress and the Catalog Card Corporation of America (CCCA). When establishing an account, the library media specialist will be required to complete a profile of the center's cataloging practices and select options that most closely match. The library media specialist must evaluate cost, convenience, and timeliness in filling orders. LC card sets are less costly but require manually adding the headings to each card; CCCA provides file-ready cards. LC will maintain back orders in hopes of filling them at a later date; CCCA ships only available card sets, which might require submitting orders more than once. Using a catalog card processing service will require submission of a separate purchase order or requisition.

Another option for obtaining catalog cards is through OCLC, a centralized cataloging computer system located in Ohio. OCLC provides efficient service to customers processing large quantities of books, but the cost is prohibitive for individual schools. Also, OCLC uses Library of Congress subject headings, which are not always compatible with the existing headings in a school catalog. Especially at the elementary level, *Sears* headings are preferred as LC subject words may be too sophisticated for the students.

Schools with an automated catalog enter data directly into the computer from the verso of the title page. When computerized circulation and inventory systems are used, the cataloging information is not entered into the computer until a bar code has been assigned to the book.

Although the verso of the title page provides both the Dewey decimal classification number and the Library of Congress classification number, Dewey numbers remain the most suitable for K–12 school use. Schools at this level do not have a multitude of exotic or in-depth subject materials that require LC cataloging as do large universities.

A shelflist card must be prepared for each book (an example is shown in figure 17). This card remains the province of the library media staff and is not available for patron use. The shelflist card has the same format as the main entry card except the shelflist card does not have an annotation. It should include tracings so that, if a book is lost or withdrawn from circulation, all the catalog cards can be pulled.

The shelflist card has the accession or copy number written in the space where the annotation would be found, that is, in the middle of the card. Commercially prepared cards may require use of a duplicate main entry card as the accession card, forcing the listing of inventory data on the back of the card. Although the decision to use accession numbers or copy numbers is usually made when a center opens, it is possible to change at any time. The accession or copy number identifies a book as a unique entity even though multiple copies exist. There are advantages and disadvantages to each system.

Accession numbers can be affixed with a repeating number stamp. At the end of every processing session, a notation is made of the last number used or the next number to be used. A number is assigned to each book regardless of whether it has multiple copies or not. Accession books, in which the accession number, title, author, date of purchase, and price are recorded, are no longer used in most centers. This record is an unnecessary duplication of effort as all relevant information appears on the shelflist card.

Use of a copy number eliminates the necessity of marking each book with a consecutive number. A book without a number is assumed to be copy 1. A problem arises when duplicate copies are ordered and a notation is not made on the order sheet. If the new book gets onto the shelf without a copy number and both copies circulate, it is impossible to verify that a lost or overdue book is the responsibility of a specific student.

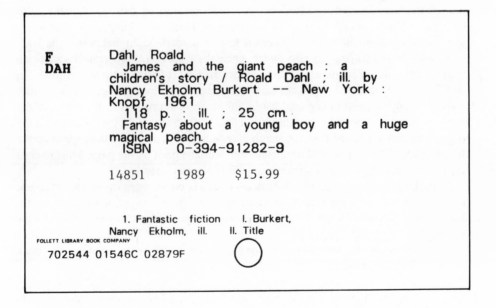

Figure 17. Shelflist card

Other information on the shelflist card includes year of purchase, cost, and (where necessary) special funding source. Gift materials are so noted, and a replacement value is assigned.

Use of a computerized circulation system eliminates the necessity for a shelflist card although many centers keep their shelflist as a back-up. The bar code affixed to each book identifies it as a unique item in the computer. Year of purchase, price, and funding source are entered into the data base for each specific item.

Processing the Book

Manual circulation systems are based on check-out cards signed by the user and retained in a library media center file. A pocket is needed in the book to hold the card when the book is on the shelf and available for circulation. Both card and pocket must identify the book by author and title. The accession number or copy number must appear on both card and pocket. When a book is returned from circulation, matching these numbers confirms that the correct card is replaced in the book. Listing the price of the book on the check-out card saves time if the book is lost and the student needs to be informed of the charge.

Some card pockets have preprinted date-due spaces. If not, a separate date-due slip must be attached. Most library media centers place the pocket on the inside of either the front or the back cover. The harder surface of the cover is preferred to the fly sheet as it is more permanent and less easily removed.

The accession or copy number is marked in the book on the title page, usually under the publisher's imprint at the bottom of the page. This number is used both for inventory and for identifying the book if someone should remove the card.

A computer circulation system does not use cards, pockets, and accession or copy numbers. Each book is individually identified by its bar code and the computer automatically assigns the due date and matches the transaction with the borrower (see chapter 4). A date-due slip is needed, however, to alert the borrower to the return date.

No matter which type of circulation system is used, the book must be identified by the school name in case it should be lost. A stamp bearing the school name, with complete address, should be used for this purpose. Books are stamped in at least two spots, although some library media centers choose to mark additional areas. The book is stamped on the title page, usually under or near the accession number, and on an inside page to make identification easier should other evidence of ownership be destroyed. In books with more than 101 pages, the stamp is used at the bottom of page 101; in smaller books, on page 51, and in unpaged books, on a right-hand page near the center of the book. If the page selected has an illustration that would be marred by the stamp or if the page is too dark for readability, the stamp may be placed at the top of the page or on the facing page. The stamp should never interfere with the print on the page. Most readers are not aware of the stamped information if it is placed correctly.

A third, highly recommended identification area is on the edge of the closed pages, either at the top or on the side. Unfortunately, some books, especially picture books, haven't enough pages for the stamp to fit. Also, if the page edges are tinted, the ink may not show.

Book detection identification strips or labels are added before making the book available for circulation.

Many library media centers feature a display of new books to encourage students' interest. Teachers should be notified when new books have been processed and are ready for use.

Paperback Books

Cataloging

Nonfiction paperback books that are substantial in content and made with quality paper are usually treated as hardback books and fully cataloged. Fiction paperbacks and less sturdy nonfiction paperbacks are often cataloged in less detail than hardbacks as their life expectancy is generally shorter.

Purchased cataloging is seldom available for paperbacks. When it is available, it may be too costly to be justified for these low-budget items. This means that most paperbacks need to be cataloged at the school, unless district cataloging is available.

The extent of cataloging for a paperback may vary, but the only essential elements are the call number, author, title, and (for nonfiction) general subject heading. Three catalog cards (author, title, and shelflist) will be made for a fiction book with nonfiction adding one subject card. The same standards apply to a computerized catalog; only the essential data is entered.

The key to deciding the extent of cataloging for a paperback book is anticipated circulation period. Most paperbacks will not survive extended use. The library media specialist must decide how much cataloging is valid given expected use.

Processing

Processing follows the same format as that for hardback books except that regular accession numbers are not used. Accession numbers specifically for paperbacks, such as PB101, or copy numbers may be assigned. Some designation is needed to track multiple copies of the same title and to differentiate paperbacks from hardbacks.

Preparation for circulation is completed as detailed previously for hardback books, but one additional step may be added to preserve the book through multiple handlings. The cover of a paperback book begins to show wear with the first circulation and, as the cover deteriorates, the inside pages are likely to sustain damage. To preserve the paper cover, many specialists encase it in clear contact paper. Others use a special binding machine that loosens the glue on the spine permitting separation of cover and contents. The cover is then laminated and reattached using a stronger glue. The specialist must decide whether the additional time required by this step is worthwhile. The amount of the book budget and anticipated usage are determining factors.

Audiovisual Materials

Cataloging

Audiovisual materials are cataloged as fully as books. Catalog cards may be available from the vendor, often at no charge. These card sets are valuable even if a computerized catalog is used because all information is readily available for inputting into the data bank. Plain catalog cards, like those used for print materials, may be used, or color-coded cards may be used to alert patrons that the item is nonprint.

The decision to use Dewey decimal classification system numbers or accession numbers for location markers varies from school to school. Dewey decimal numbers are necessary when audiovisual materials are interfiled on the open shelves with books. Dewey numbers are helpful even when items are shelved separately as all materials on a given subject will be shelved together.

The primary reason for not using Dewey decimal system numbers is space. Audiovisual materials vary greatly in size and shape and a single Dewey decimal system classification may include such items as captioned filmstrips, books, videotapes, and models. To accommodate this diversity, all shelves must be wide and deep. Specialists in centers that were designed for this type of storage are fortunate and should take advantage of the situation.

When space is not abundant, audiovisual media are housed separately from the print collection, either in an open area of the library media center or in a storage area. Again, library media center design often will dictate space arrangements. Materials are generally stored separately by type to make the most of space restrictions. For example, all cassette tapes are placed together in a cabinet, all records in a record holder, and all videotapes on a rack or shelf.

When Dewey decimal system numbers are used, each category must be rearranged when a new item is added. This is time consuming and often not possible unless full staffing is available. Accession numbers, on the other hand, permit new materials to be added with no rearrangement. This latter method often results in teachers or students spending additional time searching for subject-related media. There is no best answer to the cataloging dilemma. The library media specialist should make decisions based on district recommended procedure, facility design, school program, and user needs.

Processing

Preparing audiovisual materials for circulation involves marking each item with its Dewey or accession number, stamping the school identification on all parts, and making a check-out card or applying a bar code. The information is then entered in the computer or the catalog cards are filed.

Each component of a set, as well as the larger container holding the parts, should be marked with location number and school name. This will facilitate return to the center should a component be separated from its container.

Manual check-out systems are card oriented and, whenever possible, a card should be prepared for the item. A circulation card of a different color may be used to call attention to the fact that the item is nonprint. A pocket to hold the card may be attached to the box lid. The inside of the box is preferred since, when the card and pocket are placed on the outside, they are subject to excessive wear and possible loss. Some items may not need a pocket as the loose card can be placed inside.

Single filmstrips are difficult to card as they are so small. Today, few library media centers circulate single filmstrips as separate items. Those that do handle the situation in various ways. Some have cards available at the check-out desk and the borrower signs one card and lists all filmstrip numbers being checked out. Other centers package the filmstrip in a plastic hanging bag and put the card in the bag. There are many methods for handling small audiovisual items and any system that works is acceptable.

Audiovisual Equipment

Processing

Each piece of equipment should be permanently marked for identification as soon as possible after it is received. Most districts have a system to handle this, including staff assigned to do the job. A small district or private school may not have a systematic approach and it falls on the library media specialist to oversee this task. Minimally, the school location number, a number identifying the type of item, and a specific piece number are included. For example, 606-30-02 would refer to a specific school (606), the type of equipment (a filmstrip projector, 30), and the unique number of the projector (2). The district name or number may also be included. A metal plate can be attached to the item or a stylus can be used to engrave the information.

After the inventory number has been assigned, it is used as a circulation number. An inventory card is used for card systems or a bar code is attached and the appropriate information entered into the data bank of a computerized system.

Supplies

Most equipment has associated supplies that should be kept on hand to ensure continuous operation of the equipment. Projectors need replacement globes and exciter lamps, which vary with different models as well as with different types of equipment. The bulb numbers of new items should be checked and compared to available stock. It is possible to obtain a list of interchangeable bulb numbers that can be substituted for each other if necessary, without damaging the projector. Library media specialists can check with their local supply source to obtain such a table.

Computers, copy machines, and microform printers all require paper and, in most cases, this paper is not interchangeable. Copiers and microform printers may also require chemicals for the printing process.

Cassette tape players require batteries if they are intended for use away from a power supply. Other items requiring batteries may be camera equipment and cordless microphones. Each piece of equipment should be checked when it is delivered to the library media center to determine the supply item(s) required to keep it functional. This information should be recorded on the inventory card or in the computer so that it is readily available when needed.

Summary

Account control procedures are necessary to accurately track purchases and expenditures. A file is organized to hold all paper copies of documentation relevant to a specific budget. Account control sheets or computerized spreadsheets record transactions and maintain balances. Accounts must be kept current as orders proceed through the purchasing process. As items are received they are processed and made shelf ready. Processing may occur at the district or school level or may be purchased from the vendor.

CHAPTER 9

Materials Catalogs

A catalog, either manual or automated, is a standard tool in every library media center. It is the key source that assists patrons in locating information. The catalog should help the user find every item in the library media center except ephemeral materials and equipment.

Historically, card catalogs were the most practical way to gain access to the collection. Recently, however, computers have begun to replace these traditional files. This chapter will consider both card and automated catalogs in the context of the school setting along with other materials catalogs of interest to the library media specialist.

Card Catalogs

The card catalog is that box of drawers immediately visible on entering the library media center. Each drawer contains cards that provide the user with information about materials in the library media center. These 3″ × 5″ cards are filed alphabetically and are held in place by a metal rod that extends from the front to the back of the drawer. A movable metal plate, positioned behind the last card, keeps cards upright when the drawer is not filled to capacity.

Catalog Card Organization

Most library media centers have a unified catalog, that is, all cards (author, title, and subject) are interfiled in alphabetical order. This is the preferred practice for elementary and secondary school library media centers. Some universities and other libraries having extensive collections use a divided catalog with author and title cards interfiled and subject cards arranged alphabetically in a separate location. A divided catalog is more confusing than helpful in a school library media center and should be avoided.

The drawers of the card catalog are marked on the outside to help users narrow their search. At the elementary level, drawers are marked as simply as possible, preferably with single letters only, such as *P–Q, R, S*. When one drawer will not hold all cards beginning with a single letter, the division should be clear with no more than two letters used, for example, *S–Sl,* and *Sm–Sz*. Secondary schools having large collections must, of necessity, divide the cards more extensively. Drawers can be identified by groupings of three letters, but should never exceed three, for example, *Bri–Byz*.

Ideally, each drawer should be filled approximately three-quarters full of cards. The drawer should never be so tightly filled that it is difficult to read a card. The metal back support should be placed about $1\frac{1}{2}$ inches behind the last card when the cards are pushed together in an upright position. This allows the cards to tilt backwards at an angle most comfortable for the searcher to read.

Filling drawers less than half full is not efficient. Only in drawers devoted to less frequently used letters, such as I or J, should this occur and then only if it is not reasonable to combine several letters. This situation occurs primarily in small collections. Whenever a new letter begins it should be identified by an alphabetic guide card with a tab raised above the level of the 3″ × 5″ catalog cards. These may be purchased from a library supply outlet.

Subject heading dividers in the drawers of the card catalog are useful for helping a student narrow the area for searching. These dividers can be purchased with preprinted headings from a library supply firm. The library media specialist decides which subject headings to use and which to omit from the card catalog. Any subject headings that are frequently used should be included.

"See" cross-reference cards are an important addition to a card catalog. These cards direct students to the correct subject heading where they will find information. Even library media specialists are occasionally uncertain as to the approved subject heading, hence the need for *Sears List of Subject Headings*. Students, however, do not usually have access to such a guide and must find all information through the card catalog. The time spent in making "see" cards will be saved in time spent answering questions from students about why they cannot find anything on a particular subject. It will also reduce the frustration of students who are searching the card catalog for a subject they know is there, but are unable to come up with the correct nomenclature (for example, Cars—See Automobiles).

"See also" cards are valuable at the secondary level, but less essential at the elementary level. These references may confuse students unless they clearly understand the purpose. When staff is not available to prepare both "see" and "see also" reference cards, focus should be on incorporating the most used "see" references. Adding a "see also" reference, rather than relabeling all previously filed cards, saves time when usage dictates a change in subject headings.

Filing Cards

Filing catalog cards is a tedious, time-consuming task, but an essential one if students are going to use this resource successfully. Though the library media specialist ultimately is responsible for verifying that cards are correctly filed, initial filing can be done by paraprofessionals or student assistants.

When the card catalog is in good order, the specialist simply adds new cards as materials are received and deletes cards as items are removed from inventory. (Removal of cards is discussed in chapter 10.)

Usually, packets of cards are received with each new item. Cards for books with purchased processing arrive tucked inside the book's pocket and cards for audiovisual materials are packaged in a tissue envelope placed inside the box. With local cataloging, the shelflist, main entry, title, and subject cards for a single item are all generated at one time. District processing may result in cards being placed with each item or it may mean that a stack of cards for an entire order may arrive at the school library media center in filing order.

Card sets include the shelflist card. This card should be removed from the packet and prepared for the shelflist file (see chapter 8).

When catalog cards are processed outside of the school setting, someone other than the library media specialist decides to what extent cataloging will be done and how many cards will be made. However, unless district policy specifies that all cards received must be incorporated into the catalog, the specialist may decide not to include all cards. When cataloging is done in the school, the specialist chooses the headings and only those cards are made. Regardless of the source of processing, if a decision is made to limit the kinds of entries included in the catalog then that operating procedure should be stated. Generally the procedure should identify the type of entry not being included in the catalog, for example, "joint author cards not included in catalog."

At the elementary level, including cards for joint authors of nonfiction books may be more confusing than helpful. Most students will never refer to such cards and the only reason for including them is for teaching purposes.

At the secondary level, cards for illustrators may be superfluous except for art books or if the illustrator is well known. Elementary schools, as a rule, file cards for illustrators of picture books because the concept is taught at this level.

Both levels may delete either the title or the subject card when they are exactly the same (for example, SNAKES as the subject for a book entitled *Snakes*). No matter how many additional books have this subject heading, these two cards will always be filed together; therefore, elimination of one saves space. More important, users will not be misled into thinking that there are two books available.

Whenever a card is removed from the filing process, the tracings on the shelflist card should reflect that change. A line drawn through the tracing reference will save effort when the cards are eventually removed (see chapter 10). If there are no tracings on the shelflist card, the adjustment is made on the main entry card.

Cards normally are filed for a number of items at one time rather than each time individual sets are received. The time needed to file batches of cards is proportionately less because a single drawer may receive several cards, eliminating much wasted movement.

To file cards most efficiently, they should be alphabetized. This task can be handled quite well by students. Although not absolutely essential, a card sorter makes this job quicker and easier. A sorter specially designed for cards is preferred to one designed for papers. The dividers should be no more than 4 or 5 inches deep; some sorters have dividers that are 10 to 12 inches deep, making them more difficult to manipulate.

Initially, all cards are sorted by first letter only. This simplifies the alphabetizing chore. If small numbers of cards fall under each initial letter, the cards may be completely alphabetized at this point. If many cards begin with the same letter, the card sorter is used again to divide cards by the second letter. Usually by the second or, at most, third sort, the cards can be arranged in full alphabetical order.

After a batch of new cards has been fully alphabetized, it is ready to be integrated into the card catalog. Again, students, volunteers, or paraprofessionals can perform this task. No matter who interfiles the cards into the catalog, however, the cards should be placed on top of the rods. Even when the library media specialist does the filing, this is a safeguard against misplaced cards.

A copy of *ALA Filing Rules* is helpful for the library media specialist. It includes the general rules for omitting "a," "an," or "the" and for filing "something before nothing," as well as many more specific rules.

Specialists should consult the rules before filing subject cards dealing with historical time periods. EUROPEAN HISTORY and U.S. HISTORY are frequently used with subheadings. These subheadings are not filed alphabetically, but chronologically. For example, U.S. HISTORY—REVOLUTIONARY WAR precedes U.S. HISTORY—CIVIL WAR. In addition, dates appended to historical subheadings may overlap and cause confusion in filing. For these reasons, and because the library media specialist may not be familiar with the historical chronology of all countries, the filing rules are essential for a well-organized catalog.

The dilemmas of catalog card organization are most apparent at the secondary level. Elementary library media centers usually have few nonfiction books dealing with specific historical periods for countries other than the United States. Even in U.S. history, most elementary books cover major time periods rather than specific events.

If a card is found to totally duplicate one already in the catalog, the duplicate does not need to be filed. The catalog card tells students only that the library has a specific item, not the number of copies available. (Multiple copies are noted on the shelflist, however. If duplicate card sets are found in the catalog, the specialist should make sure the shelflist has been updated and the new items are additional copies.)

Sometimes, especially in long-established centers, when a new copy of an item is purchased, the old copy is retained. As the cards are filed, the specialist may discover that, although both items are the same, different catalogers have given them totally different Dewey decimal numbers. If this occurs, the specialist can either recatalog the old item to conform to the new designation or file both sets of cards. Recataloging involves pulling the item and changing the spine number, the card, and the pocket (which must either be relabeled or pulled out of the item and replaced). The shelflist card must also be changed and the old cards pulled from the catalog. This is the preferred method, provided sufficient staff is available.

Interfiling both sets of cards makes both items accessible although they will be in two different locations. This can be a problem if the student is searching for a particular author or title and stops looking in the card catalog after locating the first reference. If that item is not on the shelf, the student assumes none is available and does not look further. Fiction should not be retained with two author designations, for example, Twain and Clemens. Nonfiction, where this dilemma occurs more frequently, is less of a problem.

These and other filing problems may be discovered as the library media specialist checks the cards that have been filed above the rods. Any incorrectly placed cards can generally be refiled quickly. After all new cards are correctly interfiled in a drawer, the library media specialist pulls the rod and drops them into place. The rod is pulled either by turning the knob on the front of the drawer counterclockwise until it pulls out or by releasing a lever located on the bottom of the drawer just under the front face. The lever is pushed to the right or left with one hand while the rod is pulled with the other.

Renovating a Card Catalog

Unfortunately, many card catalogs are not totally accurate. Cards have been misfiled, cards remain for materials that are no longer available, and some materials have no cards at all. A new library media specialist may be overwhelmed by this problem, which has undoubtedly resulted from many years of neglect.

There are two ways to handle this situation: ignore it or fix it. Ignoring it is the most frequently chosen option, but this does a disservice to everyone. Users cannot rely on the catalog and become frustrated when they must use it, and the library media specialist feels guilty every time an attempt is made to teach students to use the catalog. Eventually it is necessary to bring the catalog up-to-date. This section discusses where to begin and how to accomplish the job while continuing to have a functional catalog.

Renovation must often be juggled with an already busy schedule, so the procedures recommended here can extend over long periods of time. The amount of clerical help available will be a prime factor in speed of accomplishment. Unfortunately, the less clerical help available, the more likely that the card catalog needs total revision.

The only tools needed for updating the card catalog are extra catalog drawers, paper clips, and rubber bands. An extra empty card catalog is ideal for this project. One may be available in districts where schools have closed or where old furniture is saved. If an extra catalog cannot be found, it may be possible to condense the existing catalog by completely filling the drawers and using the resulting empty drawers for beginning the reorganization. Another option is to use metal filing boxes for a temporary card catalog.

The first step in the updating process is to weed and take inventory (see chapter 10); however, a complete inventory of all holdings is not desired. Begin with a small section of the collection, perhaps one shelf. While checking the inventory, pull the shelflist cards for those materials that are physically present on the shelf. Cards for missing items are kept in the old shelflist drawer.

Remove the matching card sets from the catalog for all the shelflist cards that have been pulled. All tracings for each item should be found, if possible, and each set clipped together with a paper clip or rubber band.

Next, check each set to make sure that it is complete and that all cards do indeed refer to the same item as the shelflist card. Those sets that are totally correct are refiled with the shelflist cards segregated into a new shelflist catalog and the catalog cards filed into the empty catalog drawers.

Card sets that are incomplete or that have inaccuracies are put aside. When a small group of problem cards has accumulated, deal with them and then refile the sets. It is better to handle anomalies as they occur in order to avoid becoming overwhelmed with the task.

Because card catalog rejuvenation is a slow process that will take at least one year, if not two, it is important to alert students and teachers to the situation. Labeling both catalogs is essential and a poster prominently displayed can illustrate how to use the catalog(s) during the renovation period.

Cards for new materials are integrated into the updated catalog as they are processed. Accuracy in the new catalog is of prime importance and cards should be checked and rechecked before insertion on the rod.

When drawer space is at a premium, the contents of the drawers will have to be shifted as the updated section grows and the original catalog shrinks. Drawers must be labeled, but these can be temporary labels written with marking pen on nonpermanent, self-stick labels.

Eventually, the inventory and transfer process will encompass the total collection. At this point, the inventory starts again with the remaining shelflist cards. The objective is to locate materials that were not on the shelf during the first search. This process should be repeated several times as additional materials will be located each time. The final round should occur at the beginning or end of the school year when all materials are checked in and accounted for on the shelves.

Finally, shelflist cards for materials that have not been accounted for are combined into one or two drawers and labeled "Missing (year)." The cards remaining in the old catalog are discarded. This is not usual practice for cards of missing materials (see chapter 10), but is done only with a catalog that has suffered extreme neglect over a number of years. Although a few of the missing items may surface in the years ahead, most will never reappear. Of those that do, many will be old and will not be reintegrated into the collection. Therefore, to sort and save the cards remaining is not efficient. If necessary, it is not difficult to recreate a complete set of catalog cards from the shelflist card.

Total card catalog updating is not a project to be undertaken lightly. It requires a great deal of energy and time; however, it can be done, and the result is an accurate card catalog that better serves the students and teachers of the school.

Computerized Catalogs

Although public libraries have been converting to the computer en masse during the last ten years, school library media centers have not converted to automated catalogs as readily. This does not mean that school library media specialists are less knowledgeable or more traditional than public librarians but, rather, that they operate in a different environment and under different constraints.

The three factors that must be considered before automating the catalog are money, time, and need. A computerized catalog is much more expensive to adopt than an automated circulation system. Most catalogs run from a centralized minicomputer or mainframe and decisions to purchase these items are almost never made by the library media specialist alone. A microcomputer can be used with a networked hard disk drive, but it may lack some of the potential of the larger system—accurate feedback of item circulation status or interlibrary loan information, for example. Time is another factor to be considered. Entry of data is a long process that requires staff above that needed for normal operating functions. Finally, but most important, the need to automate the catalog should be a prime consideration.

Decision-making Process

Even when money and time are not stumbling blocks, the decision to convert from a card system to a computerized system should not be made hastily. Needs must be assessed, software and hardware must be selected, and the problem of retrospective conversion must be considered before plans are finalized.

Needs Analysis

The specialist should determine how the change from a card catalog to an automated catalog will benefit the library media center. Of major importance is what the automated catalog must do to be more efficient and effective than the current system. User needs must be analyzed and the implications of how an automated catalog will fill those needs better should be considered. The present state of the card catalog is another factor. A new school with no existing catalog, a school with an up-to-date catalog, and a school with a catalog filled with obsolete cards will each view the implications of change differently.

Software and Hardware Selection

Because of costs, selection of the on-line catalog program and the hardware that will run it is seldom done at the building level. Decisions leading to implementation of an automated system are most often made at the district level.

A networked system operating on a minicomputer or mainframe has the capability of reporting current circulation status of an item located on-site and records of other district schools or the public library having the same item. Interlibrary loan is a district option for those using a networking program.

There are numerous choices to be made in selecting the catalog program and the system that will run it, whether it be a hard disk microcomputer, a minicomputer, or a mainframe. Consideration should be given to ease of use for the age group in the school, response speed, the program's capability for accepting spelling errors, accuracy of response to input, and ease of adding, deleting, and correcting data.

Concurrent consideration must be given to how equipment failures will be handled. Even the most stable systems occasionally have down time. The specialist needs to decide how students' needs will be met during these inevitable failures.

The number of terminals to be installed has definite implications for utilization, and may require additional conduits and minor remodeling.

The automated catalog must have a back-up system. This may be stored on floppy disks, a videotape recorded directly from the computer, a printed copy, or shelflist cards and may be kept at the school or at a district site.

Retrospective Conversion

Once the decision has been made to automate, the library media specialist must decide how the current card catalog will be converted. This decision again is influenced by time and money. To totally convert an existing card catalog to a computer catalog will take much longer than inputting data for a circulation system. A circulation system requires only author, title, call number, and bar code. A catalog system requires those four items plus place of publication, publisher, copyright date, number of pages, reference to illustrations, an annotation, and tracings. Series, illustrator, and joint authors add to the amount of information to be processed.

Because of the time and personnel involved in conversion, many specialists decide to input new materials, retain the old card catalog, and gradually update the automated system. Other specialists decide to do a complete conversion and take a year or more to transfer all information before making the automated catalog available to students.

Regardless of which plan is used, eventually all holdings are transferred to the automated catalog. The specialist must then decide whether to keep the card catalog, which contains information on all older materials, or discard it. At some point, the card catalog becomes a dinosaur because it has not kept pace with new holdings, but for many years it does retain some of its value. The specialist must decide if keeping it will deter students and teachers from learning to use the new system.

Implementing an Automated Catalog

Materials cataloged for an automated catalog should be in Machine-Readable Cataloging (MARC) format. The individual entering the data must know the *AACR2* cataloging rules as materials are entered somewhat differently for an automated catalog than for a card system. Retrieval should be possible regardless of entry format.

"The multiple retrieval feature of a computerized catalog makes it possible to include as many cross references as necessary, with new references added according to expressed patron needs."[1] In the initial entry, subject headings should be standardized according to *Sears List of Subject Headings*. Unique and customized headings can be added after the automated catalog is in use and the need becomes apparent. This is one way to make the catalog responsive to local need.

After the hardware and software have been installed and tested, it is time to teach students and teachers to use this new tool. Children, generally, are eager to use an automated catalog and have no fears. Although many teachers are less computerphobic than they were a few years ago, some may be uncomfortable with the new format. Training of faculty and students should be done in an interesting way to get them excited and involved in using this tool. Demonstrations, wall charts, laminated user cards, and hands-on practice are all techniques that will help patrons feel comfortable as they access the catalog.

As the catalog is put to the test with daily use, the specialist should continue to evaluate the program to determine if it does the job intended, if patrons are able to use it independently most of the time, and if it is faster and easier to keep current than the card catalog.

Card versus Automated Catalog

Both card and automated catalogs have positive and negative features. Neither is perfect and the specialist must decide which is most appropriate for a given library media center.

In most schools, card catalogs are the existing tool. They represent a substantial investment of time and money and, if they have been properly maintained, are fully functional in the library media center setting. Conversion to an automated catalog requires an investment of more time and money. Continuation of the card catalog is relatively inexpensive as new card sets can be obtained at minimal cost. The biggest automation expenses are start-up hardware and software and conversion of the existing catalog; additional entries for new materials may be less expensive per item than cards.

The card catalog can be used simultaneously by as many students as there are drawers of cards. This is a consideration when skills teaching is done with a large group. Each computer terminal can support only one searcher at a time, a disadvantage when classes are involved with research and learning library skills.

The fact that the card catalog is a familiar entity is not a major consideration. Students are adaptable and are intrigued with computer applications. Their willingness to use the automated catalog, as opposed to their avoidance of the card catalog, is a definite advantage.

Accuracy and currency are often cited as advantages of the computerized system. Accuracy, of course, depends on the individual who is entering and removing the data. If the card file is properly checked by the specialist, accurate placement will occur. If the individual entering data into the computer is careful, all items will be correctly listed and the computer will alphabetize with 100 percent accuracy.

Up-to-date records are possible in both catalogs when a serious effort is made to integrate catalog information as soon as new acquisitions are processed. Information must also be deleted from either catalog when an item is withdrawn or lost. This again is the responsibility of the specialist and the format of the catalog is irrelevant. The computerized catalog, however, has the capability of reporting items temporarily missing and alerting the specialist to problems, but only if there is staff and time to record such information. Likewise, the capacity to report materials that are currently circulating is an advantage of automation, but only if the catalog program is networked to the circulation program.

A unique problem of the card catalog is the fact that over the years cards suffer from the wear and tear of many hands thumbing through the drawers. Computerized data does not appear any different on the screen after thousands of individuals have viewed the same item.

Card and automated catalogs require approximately the same amount of square footage. Although the card file is a bulky piece of furniture, it contains a compact body of information. The computer itself requires little space and contains all the information available in the card catalog. However, in order to adequately serve patrons, several computer terminals must be available along with a hard disk or access through a conduit to a mainframe computer. A writing surface is required to permit students to write down relevant information or space for a printer needs to be included.

These are the major advantages and disadvantages of card and automated catalogs. The perfect solution does not as yet exist, and the library media specialist must weigh the pros and cons of each system in making a responsible decision as to which catalog will best suit the needs of the school and its patrons.

Other Catalogs

Microform

Some public libraries have introduced microfilm or microfiche catalogs in an attempt to save money and space. This option, however, does not adequately address the needs of most schools.

Microforms are excellent for some school library functions, such as periodicals (see chapter 11), but have little validity as a catalog format in a school library media center. Inflexibility, the longer time period required for patron access, and the fact that the film must be created from an original print source all detract from the suitability of this format.

Union

School districts, especially those with cataloging centers, often have a union catalog listing all items held in the school library media centers. This union catalog can be on a computer, on printed lists, or on cards.

In case of a catastrophe, such as fire or flood, the district union catalog may be the only means of verifying the holdings of a school. The union catalog is also used to give the district supervisor a better picture of each school's holdings.

Schools having automated catalogs that operate on a mainframe or minicomputer generally can access the union catalog to locate materials housed in other library media centers in the district. The union catalog gives library media centers the option of interlibrary loan without spending valuable time trying to locate a school that might have the item. The computer screen immediately reports which schools in the district have the item the user wants.

Print

Print catalogs are almost never used for a general catalog of library media center holdings, but are frequently used for special catalogs. Preferred practice places references for all library media materials into the main public catalog, either card or automated, but supplemental print sources expand the search capability.

Many teachers do not like to use the regular catalog to locate audiovisual materials. They prefer a print catalog and, if that is not available, may waste time scanning the shelves rather than looking in the card or automated catalog.

A print audiovisual catalog has some definite advantages and, if time permits, should be considered as a supplemental catalog for audiovisual materials. The print catalog is divided into two parts, a subject bibliography and alphabetical title annotations. If this material is already on a computer, it can be quickly transferred to print. Schools without a computerized circulation system or shelflist should consider the advantage of storing this information on a disk.

A print audiovisual catalog is dated almost as soon as it comes off the press and, as materials are received after it is printed, should be frequently updated. A loose-leaf notebook with single-sided pages permits revisions or addenda as needed without necessitating a total reprinting.

A definite advantage of the print audiovisual catalog is that teachers can easily reproduce those pages containing subject areas of interest. (This is also an option with computerized systems if printing facilities are available.)

Indexes are another form of print catalog. Periodical indexes, such as *Children's Magazine Guide* and the *Readers' Guide to Periodical Literature,* are among the most common. Almost all secondary schools and some elementary schools have *Granger's Index to Poetry.* Other commonly held print catalogs are the *Play Index* and *Short Story Index.*

These print catalogs are useful tools, but, because they are printed for a broad audience, they include references to materials not available in the local library media center. To increase the usefulness of these print catalogs, the list of book or periodical titles indexed, found in the front of each publication, should be checked against actual holdings. A check mark beside current periodical titles held is generally sufficient. Indexes to books, such as *Granger's,* should include the call number beside those volumes of poetry that are actually located in the center.

A print catalog can also serve as a selection aid to increase holdings in specific areas. If a collection assessment has identified the need for more poetry books, *Granger's Index to Poetry* is a useful selection tool.

Shelflist

The shelflist is a nonpublic record of all holdings of the library media center. Its most common form is a file of cards located in a separate catalog or in metal file drawers. The rod used to keep cards in place in the public catalog is usually removed from the shelflist catalog for ease of removal and addition of cards. This file is kept in the library media center workroom or in the specialist's office. Only library media center staff members have access to it.

A computerized shelflist may take the place of cards. It is essential that back-up disks be made and stored in a safe place when this type of shelflist is used. Unless holdings are minimal, a printout of the entire shelflist has less value than duplicate disks that can be updated as necessary.

The shelflist is used primarily for inventory, for collection assessment, and for checking questions about lost materials that cannot be verified through circulation records. To make these tasks possible, the shelflist is not in alphabetical order. Instead, entries are in the same order that they are on the shelves. Nonfiction is in numerical order by Dewey decimal classification numbers and, within any given classification, by authors' names. Fiction is in alphabetical order, first by author and second, for authors having multiple works, by title.

Shelflist cards for audiovisual materials are either interfiled or filed separately by Dewey decimal classification or accession number, duplicating the system used on the shelves.

As noted earlier, the shelflist card identifies each item in the collection by copy or accession number, purchase cost and date, and any special funding source.

Summary

The card catalog is the traditional means of locating materials in the school library media center. Author, title, and subject cards are filed in alphabetical order with "see" and "see also" reference cards interfiled for patron assistance. Automated catalogs are a recent arrival on the library media center scene. Before converting to an automated system, consideration should be given to time, money, need, selection of hardware and software, retrospective conversion, and implementation techniques. Evaluation is a necessary follow-up. The library media specialist should also be aware of microform, union, and print catalogs. The shelflist is the library media specialist's record of holdings and is not available for general use, but for library media center administrative purposes only.

CHAPTER 10

Inventory and Weeding

Selection is the process that adds new and needed materials to the library media collection, inventory verifies the presence of materials in the collection, and weeding removes outdated and damaged materials from the collection.

Inventory and weeding logically go hand in hand as the two functions can be carried out at the same time. However, it is possible to take an inventory without simultaneously weeding and it is possible to weed the collection other than during the inventory process.

The first half of this chapter will consider the rationale for taking inventory, annual versus continuous inventory, and the procedures used in both a card-based system and an automated system. The rationale for weeding, factors to consider in deciding what items to weed, elements of a weeding policy, and procedures constitute the second part of the chapter.

Inventory

Rationale

The need to take a regular inventory is based on the fact that a library media center collection is not static. Materials get lost and disappear without anyone's knowledge. Even a book detection system does not eliminate all losses. If inventory is not an ongoing process, items that are lost or stolen are presumed to be in the collection, references to them remain in the catalog, and the library media specialist has no idea of loss ratio and no concept of the magnitude of loss. Collection development cannot be an organized, thoughtful process if present collection status is unknown.

When years go by without an inventory being taken, the associated problems are magnified. The catalog becomes filled with references to old materials and the specialist, unaware of the changes in the collection, cannot develop a plan for directing the growth of the collection.

Inventory, taken at regular intervals, is essential in the evaluation of the center. Although the number of items in the collection can be a meaningless figure, an accurate count is required by some standard evaluation tools. Area accreditation and other standards often ask for a numerical report of holdings. Inventory makes it possible to accurately report this data.

Annual versus Continuous Inventory

When to take inventory is the first decision the library media specialist should make. Traditionally, inventory has been done at the end of the school year or during the summer months. There is validity to this approach, as the annual inventory reflects an accurate picture of the entire collection once a year. This can be valuable information, especially if the specialist or paraprofessional is paid on an extended contract that permits inventory to be done after the regular school year ends. Not all centers operate under ideal situations, however. When an end-of-year inventory is required and extended contract pay is not available, closing the library media center during the last week of school is necessary. Year-round schools are faced with a continuous enrollment situation that makes annual inventory difficult.

There is an alternative to an annual inventory that is valid under most circumstances. This is the continuous inventory that is an ongoing management function rather than a time-specific one. Continuous inventory begins early in the school year with the specialist dividing the entire collection into manageable sections. As time is available, a small area is inventoried. Of course, many items will be in circulation and will not be on the shelf. Some materials that are inventoried in September may be missing by spring, but this is not a major problem as the missing items will be discovered during the process the next year.

An ongoing inventory can be done in two ways. In the first method, those items not on the shelves when the section is inventoried are rechecked after all materials have been returned. This method actually combines the annual and continuous inventories. The second method checks circulation records immediately after the shelf inventory is taken and assumes that most items are accounted for in this way.

The choice of inventory system depends on established district procedure, practice, and local school circumstances. Schools with year-round schedules have different needs than schools with traditional nine- or ten-month schedules. Staffing, collection size, and time constraints are all factors that influence how the inventory should be taken.

Card Inventory

The card inventory system is predicated on the use of shelflist cards and a card catalog. To begin the inventory process, the shelflist cards need to be in exact order by Dewey decimal classification and, where that number applies to more than one book, subordered by author's name. Next, the sections to be inventoried are put into the same order as the shelflist cards. This may mean reading all shelves if an annual inventory is being conducted or reading specific shelves as part of a continuous inventory.

The next step involves comparing the shelflist card with the actual item on the shelf. This step is accomplished more easily if two people work together. A student or volunteer can serve effectively as one member of the team; the other person should be a paraprofessional or professional. Call number, author, and title must match exactly on shelflist card and item. When more than one copy of an item exists, the accession or copy numbers must agree as well. Items that match are verified as being present and the shelflist card is returned to its correct place in the drawer.

Shelflist cards for items that are missing from the collection should be identified for further checking. If an annual inventory is being done, the card can be turned on end or paper clipped to indicate that the item is missing. A continuous inventory requires marking the card with a color-coded flag to denote a missing item for that year.

Missing items that are duplicates listed on the shelflist card with other copies require an additional step. The person taking the inventory makes a penciled notation of the current year beside the accession or copy number. The card is then flagged in the same way as those identifying individually missing items.

If an item in the collection does not have a matching shelflist card, and if an annual inventory is being done, the item should be removed from its shelf and put in the workroom until the inventory is completed. The card catalog is then checked to see if a main entry card exists. If it does, this becomes the prototype for the shelflist card; if no main entry exists, original cataloging must be done. Materials without shelflist cards found during a continuous inventory are listed on a sheet of paper by call number, author, and title. As time allows, the card catalog is checked for the main entry card and cards are created as necessary.

During the inventory period, the shelflist cards that have been flagged are checked several times against the materials on the shelves. This reduces the number of missing items as some that were not found the first time turn up by the next time.

A yearly inventory is completed in the fall of the year. As many items mysteriously reappear in the fall, the shelflist cards for missing items are left earmarked during the summer months. When the staff returns to the library media center, items that were returned over the summer are checked against the marked shelflist cards. The shelflist card for a returned or located item is treated as though the item had never been missing; the clip or flag is removed and the card is returned to active status. If the item was a multiple copy, the penciled notation is erased.

The specialist doing a continuous inventory uses color-coded flags as an alert for different years. Cards flagged for the current year are a different color than the ones for the previous year. As the shelves are read for the current inventory, special attention is paid to those items flagged the previous year. If the item is still missing, it is presumed to be lost.

Shelflist cards for lost and missing books are removed from the active shelflist and the year of loss is noted on the card. Cards with multiple entries are unflagged, but the notation of the year lost remains. The card remains in the active file.

In order to keep the card catalog current, the catalog card sets matching the shelflist cards of missing items are also removed. All tracings must be found for each shelflist card. When a packet of cards is completed, that is, all catalog cards belonging to one shelflist card have been located, a rubber band or paper clip is used to hold the packet together. It is best to remove the cards from the catalog by first removing the rod. This is more time consuming than tearing cards out, but if they ever need to be refiled, they will be in good condition.

Packets of cards for lost materials are retained in an inactive file for several years. Space and percentage of returns dictate how long they will be held. After several years, the cards are removed from the inactive file and discarded. Some specialists retain the shelflist card and discard all the others. Cards for materials purchased with federal government funds should be accounted for according to procedures established with the first grants. Although Chapter 2 funds are less specific than ESEA Title IVB about the purpose for which funds can be used, there is a regulation that states that funds used for a categorical purpose must follow the guidelines that accompanied those categorical funds. Therefore, shelflist cards for lost items purchased with these funds should be retained for at least seven years.

The shelflist cards of the most recently lost materials are consulted during the selection process so that the specialist knows what items may need to be replaced. Most losses occur from the newest materials. Therefore, it is essential that the specialist be aware of missing titles and evaluate the need for replacement in view of collection development priorities.

Occasionally, a year or more after an item has been lost, it will reappear. If the card packet is in the inactive file, it is pulled and the shelflist and catalog cards are refiled. If the item is a duplicate, the date penciled on the shelflist card is erased and the item is returned to circulation.

Items that reappear after the card packets have been discarded should be evaluated before being reintegrated into the collection. The specialist should decide if the content remains relevant and if the physical condition warrants inclusion. If the decision is made to return the item to circulation, it is treated as new except that the existing accession or copy number is used.

Automated Inventory

An automated catalog is not required for inventory; most circulation systems are capable of performing this task. To take a computerized inventory requires either a portable computer, one that is self-contained and can be put on a cart and plugged into existing outlets, or a wand that can store data until it is transferred into a terminal. The wand must be compatible with the computer being used.

To take inventory using the computer involves running a light pen or wand over the bar code of each item in the collection. Because the computer is programmed to match data regardless of alphabetical or numerical order, items do not have to be in perfect order on the shelves for the computer to process them. Though reading the shelves regularly to keep materials in order is good practice, it does not need to be done simultaneously with inventory.

Taking inventory with a computer can be done easily by a single individual. Inventory still takes some time because each item must be removed from the shelf, the bar code scanned, and the item returned to the shelf. The length of time required depends on the size of the collection. As each section is inventoried, the computer is capable of searching its files for items that are in circulation and can provide a printout of missing items.

An annual inventory is suggested for an automated system. It is easy for a competent student or paraprofessional to do and can be accomplished quickly with little or no disruption of the ongoing program. If a continuous inventory is taken, it is important that the items be in fairly good shelf order as a book with a Dewey decimal number in the 300s will be recorded as missing if it is misplaced with the 900s and the 900s are not inventoried at the same time. When the 900s are scanned, the book may have been replaced in its correct location and thus may remain in the missing category. To reduce such errors, after the inventory record of missing items is printed, the shelves should be searched to ascertain that these items are actually missing and were not merely overlooked in the process.

The next step is to designate the lost items as unavailable in the data base. If the items are later returned, the designation is changed and there is no delay in returning the item to circulation. Those items that remain missing after a year should be deleted from the active data base. These items may be transferred to a "missing" file or to a separate floppy disk for retention.

The automated catalog must be updated to reflect losses. This is faster than removing cards from the card catalog. Designations placed on the inventory list automatically appear on the screen, if desired, or the item may be deleted immediately from the patron-accessible data base. Restoration to active status is quickly accomplished should the item reappear.

As with the card system, the library media specialist who takes inventory with the help of a computer should use printouts of lost materials as a basis for selection. The difference, if there are no shelflist cards, is that missing items appear on a printed list. This list may be integrated in the computer with the list of titles being considered for purchase.

A computerized format is somewhat more difficult to scan for collection development purposes. Although the same information is available, shelflist cards are easier to read at a glance to see how many items are currently held on a specific topic and how these items compare in terms of content and year published.

No matter which inventory system is used, or whether inventory is taken annually or continuously, it is a necessary management function in a library media center. The specialist must be aware of the current status of the collection in order to purchase new materials that fill identified gaps.

Inventory statistics are useful in determining whether a detection system is necessary (see chapter 4). High numbers of lost items each year indicate that there is a serious collection development problem. School administrators may be more receptive to requests for a detection system when those requests are accompanied by statistics of loss ratio and replacement cost.

Weeding

Weeding is the aspect of collection development that is overlooked most frequently. Selection occurs in most library media centers on a regular basis. Budgets are appropriated and, because they must be expended within a specific period of time, materials are selected. Weeding, which removes materials in a systematic and purposeful way from the collection, is not predicated on time lines with accompanying dates.

Excuses for Not Weeding

Weeding is difficult for many library media specialists. Finding the time to do the job, having inadequate budgets to replace deleted items, and knowing that some value can be found in any item make this aspect of management traumatic for some specialists.

Time, as always, is a factor in the weeding process. Especially in collections where weeding has not been done on a regular basis, the prospect of weeding may appear overwhelming. However, just as collection development takes place over many years and focuses on specific elements of the collection, so weeding may occur over a period of time and should be systematically accomplished in manageable doses. The specialist needs to review the entire collection and determine which areas are most critically in need of weeding. In almost any library media center the 600s (technology), 900s (especially geography), and 300s (social sciences) contain the most rapidly changing and thus the most obsolete materials. Daily interaction with the collection permits the library media specialist to observe firsthand if these areas are in need of weeding.

Those areas deemed most critical are tagged for weeding the first year. This process continues until, over a number of years, the entire collection has been weeded. By this time, it is necessary to begin again, but the process should go faster as there will be fewer items in the critical stage. Collections that have been weeded regularly should not be neglected. The best scenario is one in which weeding is an ongoing, positive aspect of collection development.

Inadequate budgets complicate the concept of regular weeding. When budgets are not large enough to cover replacement costs, weeding becomes a dilemma for the library media specialist who wishes to retain a collection of a certain size. The number of items in the library media center, however, is not indicative of the quality of those items. It is never good practice to retain inaccurate or obsolete materials because students who use these items may assume that the content is accurate. The extent to which budget affects weeding is addressed later in this chapter, but the specialist should not forgo weeding and justify it by citing inadequate budgets.

Many library media specialists find it difficult to weed because they are able to see the historical value in almost any item. They rationalize that parts of the item are still relevant or that the item could give the student doing a report a historical grasp of a situation. Unfortunately, this is not how students in K–12 schools view materials. A research library may have cause to retain some dated items; a school library media center can rarely validate this practice.

Books that are popular, but damaged beyond repair, are other items that library media specialists have difficulty weeding. They like to think, "One more circulation . . . one more person will have the opportunity to read this book." In fact, damaged materials inspire less respect as they indicate an attitude that care of library media center materials is not important. Damaged audiovisual materials lose the interest of students and can be inoperative, for example, filmstrips with torn sprocket holes do not move through the projector easily.

The library media specialist must overcome the inertia generated by time constraints, inadequate budgets, and a proprietary attitude and set the weeding process into motion. Since others may never consciously be aware that the collection needs weeding, the library media specialist must be self-motivated to accomplish this task on a continual cycle.

Weeding Considerations

Weeding is a planned, thoughtful action undertaken to keep materials in the library media center current and attractive. Not all collections can be weeded in an identical way because each has unique circumstances that dictate the extent to which weeding occurs. Because of this, the library media specialist in the school is the person who should do the weeding.

It may be tempting to have an outside "expert" or agency come into the library media center and do the weeding or to turn this task over to a paraprofessional. These people do not have the necessary grasp of school climate and curriculum needs nor a concept of the collection development plan. Parents, or other community members, should never be pressed into service to weed. This can set a precedent for censorship that is difficult to overturn. Weeding, as the counterpart to selection, is a professional management process that cannot be delegated. It is the library media specialist's obligation to be aware of the status of the collection and the budget that exists for purchase.

There are two types of weeding—informal and formal. Informal weeding occurs as materials, damaged beyond further use or obviously dated, are called to the attention of the library media specialist. These items may be spotted at the circulation desk where they are removed from continued use. Informal weeding is an ongoing procedure that allows the library media specialist to handle immediate problems.

Formal weeding is a planned process that is not superseded by informal weeding. Formal weeding is part of collection development as an area of the collection cannot be judged adequate if it is composed of dated materials. The library media specialist must have knowledge of the current collection base in order to build and develop a given segment of the collection. The weeding process may focus on one area of the collection at a time. The specialist compares those areas most in need of weeding and those targeted for collection development.

Criteria to be considered in the weeding process are copyright date, content, physical condition of the item, number of circulations, and last circulation date. Weeding is a subjective process. The specialist weighs specific criteria, but the decision itself is not clear cut.

The library media specialist must be aware of the content of the collection before initiating the weeding process. For this reason, a specialist cannot undertake a formal weeding process immediately on being assigned to a center, no matter how much weeding is needed. A few items obviously may need to be weeded and these can be removed, following the context of the weeding policy. A more thorough weeding must wait at least one year to permit the specialist to become familiar with the collection and to develop a sense of the extent of weeding that is needed.

Copyright date gives the specialist an idea of the age of the contents. Some materials copyrighted thirty years previously may still have value while others less than ten years old may be outdated. Copyright date is a clue for the library media specialist to look more carefully at content.

Content should be relevant to the present world. A book stating that someday people may reach the moon may have historical validity, but gives students an inaccurate view of progress in space exploration. Content is the most critical aspect of weeding and is the primary focus. Although the specialist cannot totally review each item, skimming the table of contents and illustrations provides vital clues.

Wear and tear on items must be judged in view of budget. Materials with accurate content, but excessive wear, may need to be repaired and held together for as many circulations as possible if budget does not permit replacement. When funds permit, these items may be removed and replaced with new, attractive editions.

The weeding process requires the specialist to look at each item carefully and considerately. Torn pages, dog-eared corners, covers detached partially or wholly from contents, or excessive graffiti are all signals to the specialist that the item should be examined closely with weeding a distinct possibility.

If budgets are exceptionally small, it may be possible to mend or repair a book and make it usable once more. The cost in both materials and time of repairing the book must be compared to the cost of replacement. Certainly, minor repairs are recommended even when budgets are adequate, but more extensive repairs may be called for when budgets will not support replacement of damaged books.

Filmstrips should be examined for damage. Torn sprocket holes and scratches discourage use. Tears can be spliced and, if damage is not pervasive, special mending tape may save an otherwise useful item.

Pictures may be subject to excessive wear and tear and should be weeded frequently. Mounting and lamination help preserve pictures and, if facilities are available for these processes, the specialist should use them.

Each item being scrutinized for weeding should be checked for most recent circulation. An item that has not been checked out in five or ten years probably will not circulate in the next five or ten years. Items that have not circulated should be examined by the specialist to determine why. Fairly common reasons include appearance of the item, subject content that was once of high interest but is no longer of interest, uninteresting content, and poor selection choice.

Books, especially classics that have not circulated, should receive special consideration. Will retention increase the possibility of circulation? Is replacement needed to provide the same content in a more attractive cover? Will removal be a mistake? The specialist must know which titles fit these categories and make decisions based on valid reasons.

The number of times an item has circulated should be considered in conjunction with its last circulation date. Materials that have had few circulations and none in five years probably will have little or no use in future years. Materials with few circulations, but increasing in the last three years, may have been discovered and should be retained, at least until the section is weeded again.

No harm is done if some items, containing up-to-date information but underutilized, are left on the shelves to see if circulation really is increasing. These items should not be numerous, however. As a rule, when an item seldom circulates, it is probably not filling a need felt by students and teachers in the school.

Changing curriculum is a factor that impacts circulation and deserves consideration in the weeding process. Sections containing materials that were once heavily used, but have little current circulation, should be considered on the basis of whether curriculum changes warrant keeping the item.

Each item must be considered for retention or weeding in view of criteria and budget. There are no hard and fast rules, but a collection weeded of its outdated and worn materials will be more attractive to users. This is the reason why collection size as an evaluative criterion is not an accurate reflection of a library media center's service potential. A small collection that is totally current and attractive may better serve a school than a larger collection with outdated, dingy materials overflowing the shelves. The number of items in the collection, however, requires consideration. If many items remain after a thorough weeding, there is no problem. When weeding will decimate an area of the collection and funding is inadequate, the specialist faces more difficult decisions.

Weeding Policy

A weeding policy provides justification for and information relative to the removal of items from the collection. Without a formal policy, there may be criticism when teachers learn that items have been removed from the shelves. Those who are uninformed may confuse weeding with censorship.

A weeding policy should not be lengthy. It may be incorporated into the selection policy or it may stand on its own. The four elements that should be included in the policy are outlined in figure 18.

1. Rationale
2. Teacher evaluation
3. Disposal
4. Replacement

Figure 18. Elements of weeding policy

Rationale. The rationale for weeding specifies that weeding is done by the library media specialist to keep the collection up-to-date and in good condition. It may further explain that dated materials provide misinformation that is detrimental to the learning process, and that damaged books do not encourage students to care for or use materials.

Teacher evaluation. After the library media specialist has weeded the collection, teachers, who are experts in their academic fields, should be invited to review the items that have been weeded. This ensures that a useful or needed item will not be discarded if it is not replaceable. Occasionally, an item may be worn and the specialist intends to replace it. A teacher may have more knowledge of the materials available on that specific subject and know that newer editions are lacking in some respect or know that the item is no longer available and the original should be retained. A statement in the policy that teachers are encouraged to give input about materials designated for weeding reassures teachers that their expertise is valued.

Disposal. Materials that are weeded must be disposed of in a district-approved manner. Policy should state when and how that will occur.

A time limit should be set on retaining weeded items for teacher examination before final weeding clearance. This period should be long enough to ensure that no mistakes are made, and varies from three months to one calendar year. The retention time will depend on the number of items weeded, the storage space available, the reason for removal (damage, nonuse, dated, etc.), and the disposal policy.

Final disposal may be a book sale, donation to a civic agency, paper recycling, burning at a district facility, or some other method. District policy often prohibits the more positive dispersion of weeded materials and requires that items be disposed of in ways that will not cause the public to think that school revenues are not fully utilized. It is imperative that the library media specialist be aware of district policy and not violate it.

Replacement. Policy should include some reference to replacement, but should not promise to replace item for item. Some materials that are weeded should be replaced. These are items that have current value and that were weeded due to damage or wear and tear. Some weeded materials are available in new editions that should take the place of the original. Many items that are weeded are dated or no longer have application to curriculum or interest. These items may be replaced with other materials according to current collection need and focus.

Procedure

As an item is earmarked for weeding, it is removed from the shelf and placed on a book truck for transfer to a holding point in the library media center workroom. The initial decision to weed an item is made with a cursory evaluation done at the stack location. A more in-depth review takes place as the library media specialist looks more closely at those items pulled for weeding and as teacher consultations take place.

Those items to be withdrawn from the collection must be processed out of the system. This involves removing the shelflist and catalog cards in a card system or deleting the entry from the data base in an automated system. Catalog cards for weeded materials are not retained. However, the shelflist card or printed shelflist information should be retained for use in the selection and collection development process.

If the item weeded is a duplicate, only the reference to the specific item on the shelflist is deleted. In a card system, this involves putting a *W* (to indicate removal by weeding) and the date by the accession or copy number on the shelflist card. In an automated system, reference to the specific copy is removed from the circulation/inventory data base.

Next, the weeded item should be stamped "Obsolete" or "Discard" to indicate that it is no longer a part of the collection. The pocket and card should be removed or a magic marker used over the bar code.

Disposal is all that remains and, as has been stated previously, this must be in accordance with district policy. If book sales are permitted, weeded materials should be accumulated until a sufficient number exist to make a sale feasible. If disposal is by other means, the materials should be boxed and labeled for pick-up by the responsible district department. Disposing of materials in trash cans is not recommended.

Summary

Inventory is the process of accounting for the contents of the library media center. Taken on an annual or continuous basis, it ensures an accurate record of holdings. Inventory procedure matches each item in the collection to its shelflist record. Items not located during the inventory are presumed lost and, after a designated period of time, references to these items are deleted from the catalog.

Weeding is the planned and systematic removal of outdated, damaged, and unused materials from the collection. Informal and formal weeding should both be ongoing functions of the center performed by the library media specialist. A weeding policy should include the rationale for weeding, teacher evaluation of weeded materials, and disposal and replacement of items. Criteria for weeding include copyright date, content, physical condition, number of circulations, and latest circulation. Weeded materials must be removed from the system and references eliminated from public access catalogs. Disposal occurs according to district and school policy and library media center discretion.

CHAPTER 11

Periodical Storage and Retrieval

Periodicals are published primarily as ephemeral items. That is, they are not printed with permanence in mind but rather, as information media to be read and discarded.

Libraries of all kinds view periodicals from a different perspective than the general public, recognizing that much of the content is valuable for research purposes. Material appears in print much more quickly in periodicals than in books and many items of current interest may never be covered in a book due to timeliness, relevance, or lasting value. Periodicals, therefore, offer the most up-to-date source of information and the most complete coverage of current events. Historically, they have value as primary source material. Information written in books after the fact has a different viewpoint from articles written as events are unfolding.

Periodicals are handled differently at the elementary and secondary levels because of curriculum implications. This chapter will focus on the storage and retrieval of periodicals at both levels, but with an emphasis on the needs and problems of secondary library media centers.

Organization and Storage

Due to content and the reading styles of students, periodicals must be considered as a source of leisure reading material as well as a research source. This presents the dilemma of how best to make the periodicals readily available for student perusal while ensuring their availability at a later date for research. As current issues replace the previous issues, the library media specialist must decide how to best accumulate them while making them accessible to students.

Elementary Schools

Elementary students do comparably less research than secondary students so the problem of research versus leisure reading is not as acute at this level. Most elementary schools have a periodical rack displaying the most current copies of each title. These may be placed in plastic covers if students read current periodicals extensively and if sufficient funds are available to purchase the covers.

Back issues at this level are often kept on the display rack, housed in an easily accessible section of the periodical stand or placed in storage boxes adjacent to the display area. Circulation of back issues depends on future needs, collection size, and the extent to which using a periodical index, such as *Children's Magazine Guide,* is taught.

Retention time for back issues depends on space, use, and condition. Minimally, two or three years' retention of back issues is considered adequate. If there is storage room, optimum retention is no more than five years. Beyond that time, information is not current enough to warrant the space required for storage.

The one periodical most retained by elementary school library media centers beyond a two-to-five-year period is *National Geographic*. Many library media specialists believe that the content value of this periodical exceeds that of other periodicals. This may be true for articles on animals and other relatively unchanging subjects, but a problem may occur if fifty-year-old copies are used for reports about countries and people or other rapidly changing topics.

The amount of use back issues receive is also a factor in determining retention time. Students may continue to enjoy browsing through back issues or they may lose interest in them after a year or so. The condition of the periodical after extensive use is another consideration as retaining an issue with many missing pages is not sound practice.

Newspapers should be considered separately. It is widely accepted that all schools should have at least one daily newspaper available for student use. Because most elementary schools subscribe to only one or two newspapers at most, they generally do not use the traditional library stick holders. Instead, the newspaper is placed in the periodical rack and read as it would be in the home. Ideally, back issues should be scanned and articles cut out for the vertical file; most elementary library media centers, however, do not have sufficient staff to oversee this project, plus there is seldom a need for information from back issues. Newspapers generally are retained for a week at most and then discarded.

Retention and circulation of periodicals depend, to an extent, on the total holdings of the library media center and on the curriculum. An elementary school with an outdated print collection may find it valuable to expend a greater portion of the budget on periodicals to expand resources of current interest. Schools in which the research process is an integral part of the curriculum and frequent reports are required will also need a more extensive periodical collection.

Secondary Schools

Secondary schools approach the storage of periodicals differently than do elementary schools. There is a definite need for retention of research materials in the secondary library media center. Softcover periodicals are considered in two separate categories— those that are indexed and available for research and those that are strictly for leisure reading.

Most secondary schools find it necessary to put current softcover issues into plastic covers to protect them while in use. The decision to buy slip-on or locking covers is determined by the extent of loss due to theft and by the budget available.

Optimally, all current issues should be openly displayed. However, many library media specialists find that some high-interest periodicals disappear as soon as they are put on display. In this case, it may be necessary to retain the current copies behind a counter where students must request them so that the library media center is able to serve all the students rather than provide free subscriptions to a few. When periodicals are removed from open access, the library media specialist must advertise the holdings and the process used to gain access. A colorful display on a periodical rack showing titles and photocopies of the current tables of contents will make students aware of the magazines. A large poster should direct students to the location where the copies are available.

Back issues are retained for all subscriptions although some will be used much more than others. The length of retention depends on storage space, intended use, and other procedures, such as binding, microforms, or on-line text.

Recommended practice suggests a five-year retention period for all materials used for research purposes. Nonindexed periodicals purchased strictly for leisure reading are retained for a shorter period, usually one or two years. Whether these nonindexed titles circulate, how much they are used, and how extensively back issues are read are factors determining retention.

Circulation of indexed periodicals is a thorny question. Primarily this decision depends on how well the copies survive circulation, how much use they receive in the research and teaching process, and whether they will be bound or available in some other format.

Storage of softcover periodicals is a problem given the large number of subscriptions needed for a secondary school collection. Periodical boxes of various sizes, shapes, and colors can be purchased from library supply companies. Each box is marked with the periodical's title and the dates of the issues stored inside. Issues are arranged in order according to date of publication with the most recent being added on the right-hand side if stored vertically or on top if stored horizontally.

To make location of specific issues easier, boxes can be color-coded for each year. Inside the box, each magazine is marked on the spine with a strip of colored book mending tape matching the color on the box. The date is marked in large letters and numbers on the tape. This allows uniform placement of issue dates and permits easier retrieval and replacement.

The problem of missing issues is inherent in softcovered back issues. Unless there is constant surveillance and locked storage, copies will disappear occasionally. Removal of individual articles is a related problem.

Some secondary school library media specialists bind periodicals to ensure their availability on a long-term basis. Organizing bound periodicals on the shelves is easier than arranging softcover issues as each bound volume is identified by title, volume number, and inclusive dates on the spine.

If periodicals are to be bound, each year's accumulation of softcover periodicals is assembled after all issues have been received. This is done in January in public libraries, but schools on nine- or ten-month calendars normally wait until the end of the school year so that use of periodicals will not be interrupted.

Not all periodical subscriptions should be considered for binding. Only those with long-term interest and evidence of heavy research should be bound. Periodicals focusing on rapidly changing subjects, such as science and health, should not be included. News periodicals and those related to the arts and social sciences are more commonly retained long term. Determination of which periodicals to bind is usually made by the library media specialist in the school. The specialist should continually assess the periodicals in use and be prepared to stop binding titles that are no longer useful and begin binding new titles as curriculum changes.

Just as book collections are ever changing due to the selection and weeding processes, so should bound periodicals reflect changing needs. Periodicals in hard covers should not be considered any more sacrosanct than other print items. Weeding, however, cannot be determined book by book, on the basis of individual use. A continuous series must be maintained, but the date when the series begins may be moved forward (i.e., all issues retained since 1970 rather than 1950), or the entire holdings of one title may be removed.

Bound periodicals proliferate rapidly. One year's worth of issues from weekly periodicals such as *Time, Newsweek,* or *U.S. News and World Report* fills four large volumes. Periodical storage space is often limited and bound periodicals may usurp other space.

Binding periodicals reduces theft problems. The hard cover and more visible size make removal, intentional or unintentional, more difficult. The problem of excised articles remains.

Rather than accumulating softcover periodicals or having them bound for preservation, many secondary schools have turned to microforms. Microforms are available in either microfilm or microfiche. Regardless of format, it is estimated that periodical microforms use at least 90 percent less space than the same titles in bound form.

Microfilm is produced in 100-foot reels of 16mm or 35mm film with each reel containing approximately one year's contents of an individual periodical. The pages are reproduced consecutively, making it easy for the student to locate information. Little instruction is needed to teach students how to use microfilm; five minutes is usually sufficient. The disadvantage of this format is that, as with bound periodicals, the student must deal with the entire year's contents when searching for a single article.

Microfiche is the second type of microform selected for school library media centers and its popularity is growing. Each fiche is a card of film, approximately 4" X 6", with up to ninety periodical pages reproduced per card. Location of the exact page is a little more difficult with fiche, but the reader is easier to learn to use than the microfilm reader.

Because there are advantages and disadvantages to microfilm and microfiche, the library media specialist should be familiar with both processes before deciding to implement microforms. As both formats function equally well, there is no reason to change formats once one has been selected. Not only is it confusing to students to have two formats, it is also costly in terms of equipment.

The type of film desired should be stated when ordering periodicals in microformats. Positive film appears on the screen as the printed word appears on the page, that is, black words on a white page. If the page is printed on the reader/printer, however, the reverse occurs—white words on a black page. Negative film is just the opposite: the printed page appears as it did in the original and the screen shows white on black. Negative polarity is the most popular as the eye adjusts quickly to the image on the screen. This means that reading the screen is less tiring over an extended viewing period and the print copy is in its traditional mode.

The developing process used by the distributor is another issue. Silver halide, vesicular, and diazo processes vary from each other slightly and each has advantages and disadvantages. Any of the three is acceptable in the school setting with the only caution being not to mix film types in the same storage unit. The chemicals used to process the film in the vesicular and diazo methods can cause a reaction in the silver halide film. There is no problem with having all types as long as the silver halide is kept in a separate storage box.

When microforms are the primary source for periodical literature, sufficient machines should be made available. A reader/printer is essential if students want to do extended research. It frees the microfilm readers so that more students may have access to the resources. The quality of readers and reader/printers varies and the specialist should purchase the best quality at the lowest price.

As with other periodical formats, the library media specialist must decide which titles should be obtained in microform. It is important to be aware that, in most instances, the microform cannot replace the softcover subscription as it does not serve the same purpose and is not available weekly or monthly. Microforms are not purchased on a continuous basis; rather, they are acquired annually or semiannually. They are not suitable for leisure reading or as access to current news and information. For research purposes, they do solve the problems of space, missing issues, and wear and tear.

Microforms do not need to be weeded as frequently as print materials and can be retained as a valid historical source. The specialist should review the microform collection periodically and verify the validity of continued subscriptions to the designated titles.

Periodical literature available through computerized sources is expanding at an almost incomprehensible rate. There currently are many data bases that offer full text articles as well as some that offer abstracts. The problem with utilizing most full text resources in the school library media center is one of cost. Full text data transmission occurs through telephone communications, which means that each minute of connect time incurs telephone charges. The primary cost, however, is in purchasing periodical information in this format. Because this is a new technology, it is expensive for the vendor to build the program and initially input a significant amount of information to make it useful as a data source. As full text on-line services expand and the technology becomes more commonplace, this format may eventually replace other forms of reference storage.

Few library media centers currently feature full text on-line service as their primary periodical reference source. School library media specialists need to be aware of the potential for this technological development, but implementation at a level that will solve the back issue periodical problem is remote at this time.

In larger cities, the media may operate on-line systems that convey current news and local information by way of computer and modem. This service, because it is local, requires no long distance telephone charges and normally is free to those in the local calling area. This edited text is an excellent source of current information.

Social Issues Resource Series (SIRS) is a very useful periodical supplement for school library media centers. This ongoing subscription series consists of loose-leaf notebooks filled with reprints of articles relating to a specified subject. For example, a notebook labeled DRUGS will include up to one hundred articles all relating to the subject of drugs. As new materials are made available, supplemental packets of articles and additional notebooks may be purchased. If an article is lost or stolen, it may be replaced for a nominal fee. An index in each notebook makes finding information a simple matter. Full bibliographic data is included on each reprint.

The value of a SIRS collection lies in its complete coverage of information on a given subject, primarily social issues. More mundane issues and many current news concerns are not included in the collection. For this reason, the series cannot supplant the usual periodical resources, but serves as a supplement to them. Students who are just beginning to learn the research process can easily grasp the concept of using periodical sources by using the SIRS materials and can be led to discover the wide range of periodical literature.

Retrieval

Periodical literature as a research source is useless unless students have a tool to assist them in retrieving the information. Therefore, any library media center that retains periodicals for student use in writing reports and research papers must have an appropriate index.

Print Indexes

Elementary school library media centers, for the most part, should subscribe to *Children's Magazine Guide*. The periodicals indexed in this guide are appropriate to the interests of students in grades 2–6 and the titles included are those most often found in elementary school library media centers.

Teaching search strategy begins in the elementary grades and should include basic information for retrieving periodical literature through an index. *Children's Magazine Guide* has a format that is similar to adult indexes, but the larger type and less cryptic style make it easier to read and understand.

The *Abridged Readers' Guide to Periodical Literature* is used in most middle and junior high schools and small high schools. It indexes popular periodicals most often used for research by the lay public and is the smallest and most general index available to secondary schools. Secondary schools with smaller budgets subscribe to the *Abridged Readers' Guide* and purchase periodicals from those indexes. Although not all periodicals in a school collection need to be indexed in the *Abridged Readers' Guide to Periodical Literature,* the majority should be.

The *Readers' Guide to Periodical Literature* is the index most adults consult in their public libraries. Therefore, senior high students should have access to this basic tool whenever possible. Larger in scope than the *Abridged Readers' Guide,* it indexes periodicals of interest to the senior high school student for leisure reading as well as for research. The large number of periodicals indexed makes selection a challenge when the budget will not permit purchase of all appropriate titles. When a microformat is available, the index should be marked to indicate the titles and issues available in that format as well as those in the traditional formats.

Periodical indexes are available for many specialized subjects, but most of these are not applicable to school library media centers. Single copies may be obtained for teaching purposes, but are seldom purchased for general use. An exception may be a magnet high school with a specific emphasis of study. In those schools where there is a decided interest in a specific subject area and where the supporting journals are available, purchase of a subject-related index makes good sense.

The single most used periodical index, other than the general indexes discussed previously, is the *National Geographic* index. This resource is invaluable if the library media center has an extensive collection of *National Geographic* back issues.

Microform Indexes

Microform indexes solve some of the problems of print indexes by organizing index information in a succinct system. *Magazine Index* is one of the most used microform indexes. A single reel of microfilm can hold several years' worth of index information. The index subscription includes an index reel and a microfilm reader. The reel remains on the reader until an update is received. The single reader may limit the number of users, but the speed at which a user can search multiple years of indexing compensates for any delays. The ease in using such a mechanized index can encourage traditional nonusers to attempt the research process.

Electronic Index Data Bases

Entry to a much wider range of information is the result of new technology that is changing the world of periodical research. Electronic index data bases are expanding rapidly and each year more refinements and services are offered by the vendors. As the technology permeates public and university libraries, it is increasingly important that students develop the skills to search these sources. At present, the electronic periodical data base is both a teaching tool and a source of information in secondary school library media centers. One of the first school districts to realize the value inherent in electronic searching was the Montgomery County (Maryland) Public School System, which initiated *Dialog* searches in 1976.[1] It is possible that electronic indexes may someday replace print indexes.

Electronic data bases have several distinct advantages over traditional print indexes. First is their comprehensive scope. Whereas most secondary schools subscribe to a single print index, a subscription to a data base expands the index base to cover a wider range of periodicals and often other information sources as well. Second, an electronic data base is more current than the traditional print source because the lag time involved in the printing process is avoided. A third advantage to an electronic data base is that search time is drastically reduced. When a student has formulated a search strategy, all entries available in the selected index are retrieved. Traditional print indexes must be searched volume by volume in order to locate all available sources. Given these advantages, it would seem that all schools, especially high schools, should abandon print indexes and install electronic sources.

While all high schools should consider this sophisticated technology as a teaching tool, there are some disadvantages that make total commitment impractical for most school districts. The first disadvantage is cost. An electronic data base requires purchase of at least one computer, a printer, and related hardware. Besides the expense of hardware, there are the costs for the service itself. Another disadvantage is lack of access to the text materials indexed. This is less of a problem in cities with good public or university library collections nearby, but it is an acute problem in rural areas without access to these resources.

There are two types of electronic indexes available, CD-ROM and on-line. These will be explored briefly. The library media specialist who is interested in pursuing these technological options should consult current journal articles.

Compact Disk–Read Only Memory (CD-ROM) is the most recent technology developed for storage and retrieval of index data. It is a new technology, but its impact is rapidly being seen in public and university libraries. School library media specialists are also eager to take advantage of this technology.

CD-ROM eliminates on-line telecommunication charges and the connect time spent in actual searching. Basically, it serves the same purpose as the print index, but the great amount of storage space permits many more entries. It is updated at regular intervals as the subscriber receives new disks that contain recent information.

A CD-ROM system requires specific hardware and compatibility between disk program and player. This is yet to be standardized so that any player will accept any disk. This is the same dilemma that exists with VHS and Beta half-inch video formats, extended to a whole range of CD players and computers. For this reason, a library media specialist must choose a product and then purchase the compatible hardware. *Wilsondisc* is a newcomer on the CD-ROM scene and their products, tied to H. W. Wilson periodicals, are intended for primary searching before going to an on-line search. Another CD-ROM index presently available is *InfoTrak*. CD-ROM programs have been developed for user-friendly entry and are relatively easy for the novice to access. This makes CD-ROM application appealing even at the junior high level where search strategies are less structured. Again, however, as in all automated library media functions, there must be a sufficient number of computers and CD-ROM disks to make this option feasible.

On-line index services are those that offer search capabilities through a modem from a computer in the library media center to a large data bank located at a remote location. *Dialog* and *Wilsonline* are two on-line sources commonly used by school library media centers.

Use of an on-line data base requires the student to have an understanding of search strategy, that is, how to narrow a topic from a broad area generating hundreds or thousands of entries to the point where a sufficient number of references specifically fit the topic. To do this, the student must understand the basic Boolean operators, (AND, OR, and NOT), as well as the key operands of the system.

Using an on-line data base as the initial access point for a search is costly. To assist the student in setting the parameters for a search and to lessen on-line costs, gateway programs, such as *Wilsearch,* enable the student to formulate a search before going on-line. Gateway programs are user friendly and are designed for the student who is not a trained researcher.

An on-line data base can be accessed only by people or institutions that have established an account with the company. Upon entering a contract for services, the applicant receives a password and accompanying instructions for formatting entry procedures. Telecommunications travel through telephone lines via Telenet or Tymnet, which are accessed by a local telephone number.

Establishing on-line searching for index information incurs expenses in addition to the one-time purchase of the hardware. A communication software package must be purchased in order to connect the computer with the data base source. Telecommunication costs and on-line connect time charges, as well as the monthly telephone bills, must be taken into consideration as these items continue to generate costs as the program proceeds. On-line costs vary with the format and data base selected although some services, such as *Dialog* and *Wilsonline,* have special student rates for teaching the process.

On-line search technology, along with other computer-generated information sources, is growing rapidly and becoming more sophisticated. The focus is also turning toward procedures that will make user applications more accessible to the general public and will narrow the services available only to trained researchers. In the next decade or so, this mode of information retrieval may revolutionize search techniques and applications.

Summary

Periodicals serve a definitive research purpose in the school as they constitute the most current source of information available. They are also an excellent leisure reading source. Current issues, in general, are placed in special display racks where they are readily available for student perusal. Back issues are retained for a minimum of three to five years and longer if need demands and space permits. Options for storage of back issues are periodical file boxes, binding, microforms, on-line full text services, and SIRS.

Retrieval of information from periodicals requires an index. In print format, *Children's Magazine Guide* is the basic index used in elementary schools. Secondary schools primarily subscribe to the *Readers' Guide to Periodical Literature* or the *Abridged Readers' Guide to Periodical Literature.* Microfilm indexes and electronic data bases are becoming more prevalent in school library media centers with CD-ROM and on-line sources gaining popularity.

CHAPTER 12

Paraprofessionals, Aides, and Volunteers

A professional library media specialist is essential to an effective library media program producing optimal educational outcomes. The concepts of specialist and program are synonymous when applying Loertscher's taxonomy to the level of service offered in a school. However, the operation of a library media center is a complex endeavor that requires differentiated staffing. The library media specialist(s) should focus on providing professional services related to instruction, access to information, instructional consultation, and administration while the day-to-day routine operations should be handled by paraprofessional staff.

Unfortunately, not all schools have sufficient paraprofessional staff to handle all maintenance functions and others lack even minimal paraprofessional support staff. In these schools, clerical and operational tasks interfere with the professional ones of the library media specialist.

There are two sources of supplemental human resources available to every library media specialist: student aides and adult volunteers from the community. These individuals represent a frequently untapped source of assistance. They can provide valuable help by performing many of the daily tasks. By drawing on the available talents of students and volunteers, efficiency is increased and, as a corollary benefit, the community's perception of the library media program is strengthened.

Combining the resources of professional library media specialists, paraprofessionals, student aides, and volunteers can maximize the level of library media service available in the school. It is the responsibility of the library media specialist to coordinate and supervise these people as well as to delegate the work. This chapter will discuss how to most effectively use paraprofessionals, student aides, and community volunteers in the school library media program.

Paraprofessionals

Paraprofessionals provide a necessary support system for the library media specialist. They have a variety of backgrounds, but lack the M.L.S. or library media endorsement and teaching certificate of the professional.

It is vital that library media paraprofessionals be carefully selected and trained for the tasks they are to perform. Supervision of paraprofessionals is the responsibility of the library media specialist and is one of the professional aspects of administration.

Selection and Hiring

Library media specialists should be actively involved in the selection of paraprofessionals who will work with them. There is considerable responsibility involved in
selecting a paraprofessional who will work closely with the school's professional staff
and with the patrons of the library media center. Selection should be based on information obtained from the application, interview, and references, and should be as unbiased
as possible.

Selection of paraprofessionals is not an easy task. Most educators receive little
training in this essential process and, when placed in a position requiring this skill, feel
insecure and uncertain of how to proceed. Sufficient time should be invested in the
selection process, even if it means leaving the library media center understaffed until the
best individual is found to fill the position. This is much preferred to selecting hastily
or accepting individuals who do not meet the established criteria. Unless there is
evidence of discrimination in hiring practices in a district, a decision not to hire someone
will seldom be challenged, but once an individual is hired by the district, removal for
cause requires time as due process must be followed. Good selection is the basis of a
good team relationship and is worth the effort and time involved. The library media
specialist who has the responsibility of recommending individuals for paraprofessional
positions should look for certain characteristics.

Dependability is key to a paraprofessional. Given the job description of a library
media specialist, there is no time for constantly checking to be sure the paraprofessional
is working. This does not negate the supervisory aspect of working with paraprofessionals, but rather emphasizes the need for hiring individuals who will be dependable in their
work habits, including attendance.

Reliability is a second essential characteristic. This trait permits the library media
specialist to have confidence that when the paraprofessional commits to performing
certain tasks the jobs will be done in the proper manner.

Interest in library media work is fundamental. A paraprofessional who has no interest
in the books and materials of the library media center will probably not be motivated to
do the job well. If the paraprofessional is to have contact with students, a love of children
is extremely important. Even if the paraprofessional is to be assigned strictly to behind-
the-scenes work, it is vital to like students. The work setting involves young people, even
if peripherally, and every trip into the halls means contact with students. Enjoyment of
daily interaction with students may be a minor factor with someone who does not work
directly with them, but over the year's time, it may mean the difference between an
individual who enjoys the job and one who is disgruntled.

A position that requires technical skills will necessitate a search for someone with
specific expertise. A television technician must have knowledge of video equipment and
its use, while a clerk must have typing or word processing skills. While not widespread,
Library Technical Assistant (LTA) training programs are available that specifically train
an individual in library technical support skills. However, a paraprofessional who is
hired to assist the library media specialist as a generalist can be taught the necessary
skills; therefore, other characteristics assume priority.

The interview is the vehicle for obtaining the requisite information. Before interviewing any candidates, it is wise for the library media specialist to contact the district
personnel office and find out exactly what rules and guidelines apply to hiring paraprofessionals. Some districts leave notification of the selected candidate to the specialist,
but most districts either give this responsibility to principals or retain it at the district
level. It is imperative that the specialist adhere to district procedures.

The interview process begins by setting the candidate at ease. The library media specialist should be aware that the individual being interviewed may be nervous and may have had little interviewing experience. A few minutes spent in preliminary conversation may mean a difference in outcomes.

After the initial pleasantries, the interviewing process should get under way. For the novice interviewer, it is wise to have questions written in advance to assure that important aspects are covered. It is best to be specific in questioning and in providing information. The applicant should be told exactly what types of work the job entails, what days and hours will be required, and the benefits included. The law forbids asking questions about family concerns and other personal data not related to the job situation.

Tasks

The primary purpose of having paraprofessional staff in the library media center is to free the specialist for the professional duties that raise the level of services offered. The jobs assigned to a paraprofessional depend on the physical facility and the size of staff in relation to the size of the school. A single professional assisted by a single paraprofessional can provide a wide array of services in a school of 500 students, while the same two personnel in a school of 3,000 have time to offer only minimal services.

Schools with a diversified staff and the appropriate facilities are able to offer significant technical services. These usually involve production of original materials and may include television, computers, graphics, and printing. While these services are highly recommended, they are normally the first to be eliminated when staffing levels fall because each aspect of technical services requires a technician with specialized training and expertise.

The generalist paraprofessional is most commonly found in library media centers and is responsible for a wide variety of tasks. Circulation responsibilities include supervising the check out and check in of materials and equipment, preparing overdue notices and lists, shelving materials, and coordinating audiovisual materials received from a district or regional center. Secretarial tasks include typing orders, letters, bibliographies, and computer input. Bookkeeping skills are needed for maintaining records and accounts. Other possible tasks include inventory, one-on-one student assistance, materials processing, book and filmstrip repair. . . the list goes on, limited primarily by time and staff.

Training

Most paraprofessionals, except technicians, are hired on the basis of personal traits and general skills. Few applicants have completed an LTA training program and thus do not have the specific library media background that would enable them to step in and proceed without further on-the-job training. Even those individuals who have had some library media center experience may not have been trained properly and will need direction in following procedures unique to the specific district, school, and library media center.

Training of paraprofessionals new to the field can occur at either the district or school level. If this training takes place on a district level, the school library media specialist need only orient the newcomer to school policy and procedures. When all training takes place at the school level, the specialist may need to begin at the most basic level.

The interview session, when properly conducted, can elicit a great deal of information concerning the skills of the applicant. If the specialist is the interviewer or part of the interviewing team, skills can be incorporated into the interview. Some districts and schools, however, reserve the interviewing process for designated personnel and the library media specialist has little or no participation in the hiring interview. When this occurs, an informal information interview (or discussion) takes place when the new paraprofessional reports to the library media center to begin work.

Information concerning the knowledge and specific skills of the new paraprofessional is the first step in the training process. The library media specialist assigns initial tasks that are within the capabilities of the paraprofessional. This develops confidence and permits the specialist to assess existing skills before proceeding to new skills.

The key to training competent paraprofessionals is to help them master one skill at a time. This means that the library media specialist must take as much time as necessary to teach each skill, explaining why it is done, demonstrating how it is done, and providing direct supervision and feedback as the paraprofessional performs the task. When the task can be performed correctly without immediate feedback, the paraprofessional is allowed to work independently. The specialist then reviews the results and determines whether additional training is needed.

When the new paraprofessional has mastered a skill, the library media specialist introduces the next skill. All skills do not need to be taught immediately. In fact, if the paraprofessional will not be using the skill right away, it is best if the library media specialist waits to teach the skill until it is needed. For example, if the paraprofessional is to repair books, it is better to teach the process when there are several books that need mending. If the library media specialist demonstrates the technique and there are not enough books needing repair to provide adequate practice, the paraprofessional will not learn the skill sufficiently to proceed independently at a later date. This holds true for all tasks.

A handbook of standard procedures, compiled at the local level, can be a great help to the new paraprofessional. This can be a loose-leaf compendium explaining, step-by-step, how specific tasks are performed. Examples of cards and formats present a clear picture of what is expected. Mildred Nickel's *Steps to Service* is a concise guide that can assist professional and paraprofessional to come to an understanding of the required procedures.

The two essential ingredients for the library media specialist in the training process are time and patience. It is important that the new paraprofessional have plenty of time to learn and practice one skill before proceeding to another skill. Concepts that are old hat to library media specialists may be new to paraprofessionals and time is required before the individual fully comprehends the meaning and procedure. Patience in the training process pays dividends in the future as the paraprofessional learns to handle the requisite tasks competently.

Although training in this chapter has focused on the newly hired paraprofessional, the same steps occur when any paraprofessional is assigned to a new task. Training is an ongoing process, but is most apparent in the initial stages of employment.

Supervision

Supervision of paraprofessionals is the area where most library media specialists feel least prepared. As classroom teachers, they were seldom responsible for supervising other adults' work. The principal may be designated as the supervisor of paraprofessionals in the library media center, but principals have many responsibilities and therefore rely on the library media specialist(s) to provide direct supervision and report any problems.

Supervision means providing direction and guidance for those individuals who work at jobs under the library media specialist's jurisdiction. Training, as discussed previously, interweaves supervision into the learning situation for the newly hired. The library media specialist continues to provide leadership in the planning and execution of work and informally checks performance of all paraprofessionals at random intervals.

All library media program support staff members should have complete and clear job descriptions, systematic assessment of job performance by designated professional staff, and adequate feedback on training and personal development needs.[1] Occasionally, a paraprofessional may not perform at acceptable levels. It is best if the library media specialist corrects this situation immediately rather than waiting until the matter is critical. Taking preventative measures and discussing the problem with the paraprofessional when the situation first arises may solve the issue.

If it becomes apparent that normal corrective steps are not bringing about positive change or if the situation deteriorates, the library media specialist needs to notify the principal immediately and, as a team, they should plan a course of action. Most districts have disciplinary policies that must be followed when taking action that may lead to dismissal. Due process and legal requirements must be observed. A library media specialist should not attempt to make termination decisions, but must rely on those who are responsible for these actions.

Termination of employment is rare if care is exercised in the selection, training, and supervision of paraprofessionals. Much preferred is positive corrective action and a supportive, caring atmosphere created by the library media specialist.

Paraprofessionals have certain rights that must be taken into account when the library media specialist plans the schedule. Each paraprofessional is entitled to a lunch period and breaks according to labor laws and these must be granted. Overtime work must result in overtime pay or in compensatory time off taken within a specified period. The library media specialist usually cannot require overtime work from a paraprofessional and, if such is needed, should obtain clearance in writing from an administrator.

New employees should be informed about policies and procedures in the school as well as in the library media center, and oriented to common facilities, such as the lunchroom and rest rooms. Personal use of the telephone should be clarified to prevent misuse due to lack of understanding. Although personal calls are occasionally justified, it is wise for the library media specialist to set guidelines and to personally observe them. Specific times for starting and ending the workday should be established at the time of the interview or, at the latest, the first day that the paraprofessional reports to work. Other regulatory expectations should be clearly conveyed in a positive manner.

Library media specialists in supervisory positions should take the initiative to learn more about supervision and leadership. Knowledge of supervisory styles and problem-solving techniques can make this job aspect more rewarding for the library media specialist.

Student Aides

Students constitute the largest pool of available assistance for the library media center. Logistically, they are in school on a daily basis and, theoretically, are reliable and can be depended on to appear when scheduled. Obtaining good student aides takes time, but tapping this resource can pay dividends that far exceed the initial investment.

Proper selection of student aides must be a prime consideration if the program is to succeed. Students should have a real interest in the work they will be doing, and should be dependable and self-reliant. Students who at first glance might not appear to fit the criteria should not be overlooked. Special education students are capable of performing many necessary tasks and the status of the position may not only enhance their own self-image, but raise their status in the eyes of other students as well. Their dependability and reliability may exceed that of the traditional student.

At the elementary level, the library media specialist needs to work cooperatively with teachers to arrange a schedule that does not remove students from the classroom during critical learning periods. Many teachers prefer to release students once or twice per week rather than daily, so they do not miss too much of the regular classroom program. Others will permit commitments before or after school only. This may mean working with a large number of students in order to have consistent and trained library media help.

Obtaining student aides at the secondary level is not dependent on teacher cooperation, but on students' schedules. Recent educational reform proposals have encouraged states and districts to increase the number of required subjects, leaving the student with little time for elective courses not fulfilling specific graduation requirements. As a result, fewer students may be available to assist in the library media center.

If teachers and students view library media aide positions as inconsequential and nonacademic, they need to be educated about the parallel learning experiences that can accompany a library media aide position. They should be informed that service as a student aide provides an opportunity to build the students' enjoyment of literature and libraries. There can be expanded learning benefits with students exploring research options and materials beyond those taught in the usual class setting. For some students, the experience may be influential in determining vocational choices.

Training

There are many tasks that student aides can perform with minimal supervision after being thoroughly trained. Student age and ability must be considered when making assignments and the personal preference of students may play a part, depending on the way their available time is structured. It is important that student aides go through a training program before they are assigned regular duties. Even students who have previously worked in the library media center need a review to ensure that they remember procedures correctly.

There are several ways to handle the training of student aides. The most efficient, but most difficult, is to train the group as a whole. When it is possible to use before- or after-school hours, group training maximizes the time of the library media center staff and permits students to learn from peers as well as adults.

Individual on-the-job training is very effective and can be specialized for the student(s) assigned to the library media center at any given time. For instance, some students are taught to shelve books while others learn to set up equipment or file catalog cards. Over a period of several months, students are taught a variety of skills. Requiring students to perform the same repetitive jobs over and over is one of the quickest ways to dampen enthusiasm and accelerate dropout rates. Some tasks are seen by the students as more prestigious or fun than others and equitable distribution of these jobs is important. Delivering materials to classrooms, processing new books, running equipment, and putting up displays are often more enthusiastically performed than shelving materials and reading shelves. This means that those students who initially are taught to shelve materials need to be moved to a job that they view as having more status after a month or two. Those students who were initially trained for more prestigious tasks need to take their turn at shelving materials and reading shelves.

A third alternative for handling training involves creating individual packets that students complete at their own pace and in the order designated by the library media specialist. A record sheet lists all of the packets that must be completed by each student. After the student finishes the activities in a packet, a written or experiential test demonstrates that the concept has been mastered. That skill is then recorded in the student's file and another topic is selected. Although much time is required to set up this system, the packets can be used indefinitely, especially if the original is photocopied and the copies laminated for durability.

Tasks

The tasks assigned to student aides will depend, in part, on their ages and abilities. High school students can perform many duties that in an elementary school should be performed by adults. The library media specialist should be cautious about assigning students to work with laminating machines, paper cutters, equipment, and other potentially hazardous items.

Circulation

Circulation of materials is one area where student aides can be of maximum assistance. One aide each class period, trained to help with this procedure, can be invaluable. This is a task that students enthusiastically perform and it is one requiring an inordinate amount of library media staff time. Regardless of whether a computerized or card circulation system is used, student aides can be taught the process and can assume much of the responsibility. This not only frees the library media staff for other work, but also improves service and lessens the potential for theft since someone is immediately available to check out materials.

Processing Materials

Student aides can perform many processing chores, beginning with unpacking cartons and verifying that the contents agree with the information on the packing slip. Teams of two work well here. Students can be shown how to open books, match catalog cards, and check call numbers for accuracy. Any problems can be set aside to be resolved by the professional or paraprofessional. Stamping the school name and pasting a pocket in the book are jobs that even high school students like to do.

Students can alphabetize catalog cards and do the initial filing in the card catalog. If several students perform this task, it does not become too tedious for any one person and mistakes are caught along the way. It may be preferable to have one student alphabetize to the first letter, another student complete the alphabetization, and a third add the cards to the catalog. The cards should be placed on top of the rods so that they can be checked by the library media specialist for accuracy before being dropped into place.

When a computerized system is used, high school aides with typing skills can be taught to enter data. To prevent errors, a printout should be run of each hour's input so that it can be verified for accuracy. It is much quicker for the library media center staff to adjust errors than to do all of the work.

Vertical File

Items to be clipped from newspapers or ephemeral periodicals for inclusion in the vertical file can be earmarked by a member of the library media staff and clipped by students. If the material is on continuous pages, the students can staple the pages together. Single-column items may be glued or taped to a sheet of paper to prevent misplacement and material that is on the back of another article can be photocopied by aides. Students can locate the proper folders in the vertical file and check with a member of the staff to verify correct placement before adding the new material. Again, checking is less time consuming for the staff than locating and preparing individual items.

Equipment

In a school where teachers share audiovisual equipment, students can deliver and return the equipment, freeing teachers of this chore. When students deliver equipment, the following guidelines should be followed to prevent accidents:

1. Carts should have large castors or wheels for ease in moving and two of the castors should lock.
2. Only adults or older students should move carts and then only with extreme care and never in crowded halls.
3. Small children should not move equipment that is larger than they are.
4. The proper cart should be used for each piece of equipment.
5. TV sets should be bolted to the stand or cart.
6. TV sets on carts should be pushed, not pulled.

Students may learn how to run equipment, but few teachers request this service anymore. Most teachers prefer to serve as their own projectionists as they can vary the presentation rate to meet their needs. Threading a film onto the projector, checking to make sure that projector bulbs work, inserting a videotape into the player, and locating the correct starting frame remain services appreciated by many teachers.

If a school has video cameras, taping of many activities can be done by students. They should not be required to lift heavy equipment, nor should they be expected to hold even portable cameras in the elementary grades. However, with cameras mounted onto movable tripods and with the lightweight equipment available today, students can learn the fundamentals of videotaping, freeing the library media staff while providing this valuable service.

Other Tasks

Student aides may perform a variety of other services that make their jobs more enjoyable and fun while simultaneously eliminating nonproductive or minimally productive work for the library media staff. Running errands, such as delivering overdue notices or reminders, appeals to students at all grade levels. Audiovisual materials selected for a classroom project can be taken directly to the teacher who requested them as can materials sent to the school from a district or regional center.

General housekeeping chores, such as watering plants, dusting shelves, and straightening up the library media center may appeal to some student aides. If these responsibilities are delegated to students, staff time is saved and a more inviting atmosphere created. Bulletin boards can absorb hours of preparation time for a library media specialist, but some students truly enjoy cutting out letters and assembling the components for an attractive display. Depending on the artistic inclinations and skills of the students, the library media specialist may plan the display design and theme with students assembling the project or students may be encouraged to use their own creativity with the library media specialist's input limited to approving the plan.

Using student help with inventory is a tremendous boon. Two people work twice as fast as one with a card system. The student pulls the item from the shelf, reads aloud the author's name and the title or, in nonfiction, the call number. When the specialist or paraprofessional locates the shelflist card for the item, the student reads the accession or copy number on the item to verify it with that on the shelflist card. When a computer is used for inventory purposes, a responsible student can take the inventory alone with supervision from the library media center staff.

Older student aides can be taught to provide one-on-one orientation to the center for new students. Peer orientation introduces the newcomer to the facility and the resources in a welcoming, caring, and friendly way.

Supervision

Student aides are directly responsible to the library media specialist when they are working in the library media center, although the specialist may delegate a paraprofessional or other staff member to supervise some activities. Student aides require more supervision than paraprofessionals because they are in the center for a different purpose. Paraprofessionals, no matter how much they enjoy their work, regard their position as a job and one of the rewards of a job is the salary. Student aides receive no salary in most cases. (An exception may be a vocational training program where students are paid a token salary while they learn the requisite job skills.)

Although student aides may be "fired" if they fail to perform satisfactorily, this is not recommended practice for most situations. Student library media aides need incentives to make the position attractive and to keep them interested all year long.

Library Media Club

A library media club can be successful at both the elementary and secondary levels and, although the symbols and rewards differ, the basic elements are the same. First, there must be a purpose for the group. Providing a needed service for the school may be sufficient reason for existence, but it may be necessary to go beyond this and include other pertinent rationale. The structure should resemble other organizations in the school, and having a president and secretary gives students a sense of belonging to a "real" organization.

The library media club exists for a specific purpose; therefore, it is important that students possess certain skills before they can join. Although this may elicit an elitist attitude, it helps students focus on the purpose of the club and eliminates indiscriminate joiners. The skills required should be commensurate with the age and ability of the students and it should be possible for anyone who works hard and who really wants to join to receive the training and qualify. Indeed, there may be a series of levels through which students progress. Each higher level brings more responsibility and greater status.

At the elementary level, a library media club card carried by members designates students available to perform specific audiovisual assistance for teachers. A special button may be another symbol students earn when they reach a specific level of expertise. Secondary students are not motivated by the same symbols as elementary students and symbols should be selected by the members themselves in order to have value.

Meetings are essential if the group is to be cohesive. The meetings, however, must be meaningful and interesting if students are to retain their involvement. Guest speakers, such as local radio or television personalities; field trips to media locations; authors; or demonstrations of new and innovative equipment serve to spark students' interest. There may be a special project undertaken by the library media club each year to improve the center. Some need should be identified by the members and the goal should be to provide a solution that meets this need. Finally, there should be some type of reward for dedicated service. There are some built-in rewards of self-satisfaction, but most students also enjoy a more tangible reward. This may be given as a certificate at a recognition assembly or a special party just for club members. Whatever reward is chosen, it should be one that appeals to the students.

Course Credit

Library media clubs, which may be very effective in elementary and junior high, are sometimes less successful at the senior high level. High school students often have one major goal—accumulating sufficient credits for graduation. In this case, offering a course for credit may be instrumental in interesting the students. The course may be designed along two separate tracks depending on the needs of the library media center and those of the students. One option may be a vocationally oriented course that appeals to students who want to learn more about library-related jobs. Students taking this course learn to perform paraprofessional tasks that will provide them with entry-level skills.

A variation of this vocational offering may be geared to mentally handicapped students who can learn valuable job skills as they learn to perform the basic steps of job performance. These students benefit from a simulated and structured work situation and the experience provides them with some marketable skills that can be utilized in the job market.

A second option is a credit class designed for college-bound students. This class provides opportunities for students to learn to use resource materials more extensively than is done in the regular curriculum. It combines student-aide work with assignments planned to introduce students to a wide variety of reference works and research tools. This type of class requires extensive preparation and teaching time and these constraints should be carefully considered before implementation.

No matter which type of credit class is offered, student aides must be trained and held accountable for a measurable amount of work in order to gain the credit offered. The requirements should not be so easy that students see the class as an easy A with no effort, but the work should not be so difficult or unrewarding that students avoid taking the class. A curriculum that is both challenging and enjoyable is necessary.

Adult Volunteers

Although student aides provide effective assistance in the library media center, they have limits beyond which they cannot proceed. Students generally are available only at specific times of the day for a limited amount of time. Projects that require more time to complete must be apportioned to several students or performed by someone else. Other tasks may be dangerous for young students or beyond the scope of reasonable expectations.

When a library media center has insufficient professional and paraprofessional staff, some work never gets completed. There is, however, a large pool of talent available on which the library media specialist can draw. The resource waiting to be called on is the volunteer community.

Selection

Where does the library media specialist find individuals willing and anxious to volunteer? The first group to consider is parents. There are parents who are not holding full-time jobs and the specialist should seek out these individuals—each has something to offer. The specialist needs to know what motivates each parent volunteer, as what is gained through volunteering is intangible, but important. Parents may volunteer to sharpen job skills or to increase outside contacts. They may wish to help their child's school, but not in the classroom. They may have time constraints and hours should be arranged to meet their individual needs.

A second source of volunteer help is the senior citizen group. These people have skills and abilities waiting to be used and they can provide a vital link between the neighborhood community and the library media center. Often a retired person is the most reliable volunteer as there are no children at home to consider. Retirees may volunteer out of a need for worthwhile activities or to ease loneliness.

Many school districts are building alliances with business communities through partnership programs. A business may adopt a school and provide it with volunteers from the corporation. These volunteers continue to earn their regular salary while spending time each month assisting the school. The library media specialist needs to capitalize on the talents these individuals may offer.

Training

The training of volunteers varies from that of paraprofessionals and students as volunteers may be temporary. Motivation for volunteers is not created by a paycheck, a grade, or other tangible reward. Rather, it is an intrinsic desire to be of service and assistance to the school community.

The library media specialist should spend some time initially with a new volunteer to determine how the volunteer visualizes the work he or she would like to perform. Training should include a tour of the library media center, an overview of library media philosophy, parking information, faculty lounge and rest room locations, and school rules and policies. A handbook or manual is especially useful as it gives the volunteer concrete examples and information for reference. If at all possible, training of volunteers should be done when children are not present in the library media center. In this way, the specialist can devote the necessary time to teaching the volunteer(s) correct procedures.

The library media specialist must take time to show the volunteer exactly how to perform the work that needs to be done. Skimping on instruction may negate the work done by the volunteer if it is incorrect. Until the volunteer has established a track record for dependable service, it is best for the library media specialist to assign tasks that require minimal training. As volunteers come regularly to the library media center, training can be expanded to areas requiring more detailed explanation.

Tasks

The library media specialist who utilizes volunteers successfully has work ready at all times. There are some jobs that must be done as the need arises, but others can wait for a volunteer. Book repairs can accumulate until a volunteer arrives; indeed, some volunteers who cannot work at the school enjoy taking a box of books home to repair.

It is of primary importance to match the volunteer to the task. No matter how vital the work, it will be a successful experience only if the volunteer enjoys it and returns to the library media center again.

The scope of possibilities varies with the volunteers. These individuals may have no library media background or may be retired professional library media specialists. Recognizing the strengths and goals of the volunteers and structuring the work assignment to meet their needs will result in a positive experience for both the volunteers and the library media staff.

Supervision

Working with volunteers requires the library media specialist to have good interpersonal and supervisory skills. It is not enough for the specialist to tell a volunteer what is to be done and then disappear, expecting to come back hours later and find that the volunteer has completed the job. A staff member must be available and ready to offer guidance and direction whenever it is needed.

It is especially important for volunteers to know that they are appreciated and that their help has made a difference in the education of the children in the school. The volunteer should be rewarded in a variety of ways that will make the individual aware that the work done is important and of value to the organization and management of the library media center. Rewards need not be elaborate, but should be meaningful. Sincere thank yous are the most basic and should be used in all appropriate situations. The thank you should be specific and should include recognition of the job performed. This feedback is much more meaningful than abstract appreciation.

Small things such as occasionally providing light refreshments, taking a few minutes to chat, introducing the volunteer to the principal and staff, and sending a personal letter at the end of each semester are valued by volunteers. When volunteers have provided many hours of service, it is nice to recognize them in special ways, such as a luncheon or tea or bulletin board display.

The potential of volunteers has yet to be realized. There are many people who need a sense of worth in their lives and who have a great deal of expertise to contribute. It takes some time and effort to find these people and more time and effort to train them. Some volunteers come only once; these individuals make the library media specialist wonder if pursuit of a good volunteer is worthwhile. However, each time a faithful volunteer who regularly devotes time to the program is found, the library media center has gained reliable and dependable assistance.

Summary

Professional library media specialists are essential to good library media programs, but the professional staff needs the assistance of others to handle the routine and nonprofessional tasks.

Paraprofessionals, student aides, and volunteers all have a place in the management design of the library media center. Paraprofessionals are paid staff members selected through an application and interview process. They should be dependable and reliable and should have an interest in library media work and children. Student aides constitute a potentially large base of assistance available within the school setting. Volunteers recruited from the community are a third source of assistance in the library media center. Each individual who accepts a position in the library media center should be trained, assigned to perform tasks in line with personal abilities, supervised, and given feedback.

CHAPTER 13

Public Relations

The concept of public relations as an integral aspect of school library media programs is relatively new. The need for effective communication was not obvious during the 1960s and early 1970s when money for education was plentiful. Few educators were asked to validate their existence and support services in schools were accepted without question.

This idyllic situation began to change in the late seventies as inflation and recession became bywords of the American public. Suddenly, funds were no longer unlimited and governing school boards began to look for ways to retrench. In such situations, programs outside of the traditional curriculum became vulnerable to cuts, especially when decision makers were not fully aware of the importance of certain programs. Unfortunately, misunderstanding of the library media mission too often resulted in budget, staff, and support service reductions in the library media center.

A proactive stance for school library media programs requires the library media specialist to be committed to the practice of public relations. The public relations program must be designed to communicate both the value that the library media program provides for students and the need for its availability in the school setting. Successful public relations is a combination of program excellence and effective communication. The library media staff is responsible for actively promoting the library media program by making that program responsive to user's needs, by publicizing the benefits to be derived from using the center's services, and by exploring all possibilities for increased visibility and positive image building.

An active library media public relations program educates teachers, principals, students, central office administrators, board of education members, and the community. It changes perceptions and builds needed support and enthusiasm. As has been noted in previous chapters, preferred practice and reality may not coincide. By building support for the library media program through active public relations, reality moves closer to desired goals. Budgets, staffing, and facilities may be considered more favorably by decision makers if they understand the program and its place and value in the school system. To help these influential people become more aware of the benefits of a good school library media program, an effective public relations campaign should be planned and implemented.

Four-Step Public Relations Process

All effective public relations programs are based on the effective use of communication practices and skills. Successful public relations attempts do not occur as isolated events, but as part of an overall commitment. A successful public relations program comprises four steps: research, planning, communication, and evaluation. Incorporating all four steps is essential to an effective program.

Research

Research is a vital first step that evaluates the current situation and compares the library media specialist's concept of practice to that held by others. This process begins with examination of the program, considering strengths, weaknesses, and the resources available. Next the people served are identified. These individuals are the school library media "publics" who directly or indirectly influence the status of the library media program. There are both internal and external publics to be considered. Internal publics are those individuals within the school facility—students, faculty, support staff, and building administrators. External publics are removed from the daily operation of the school, but have a definite interest in what happens in the school—parents, board of education members, PTA officers and members, district administrators, taxpayers, and representatives of teachers' associations.

After the publics served are identified, the next step is to determine the expectations and opinions these publics have of the library media program. A survey is the most efficient method of data collection, especially with internal publics. The purpose of a survey is to compare the library media program as it exists with the expectations of those it affects. A simple survey, such as the one illustrated in figure 19, can provide much-needed feedback. A questionnaire with a five-point scale, ranging from strongly agree to strongly disagree, may generate more returns from teachers due to answering ease. This type of questionnaire is shown in figure 20.

If the program does not measure up to expectations, the library media specialist should consider how the quality of service can be made more responsive to perceived needs. If the survey reveals that the affected publics are not fully aware of the services provided, a public relations campaign may focus on the positive aspects of the program with a goal of making people more aware of those available services.

Planning

Planning involves charting a course, using the data gained through research, to influence those previously identified publics. A successful public relations event takes an extensive amount of planning. Nothing should be left to chance and careful planning averts unpleasant surprises at the last minute.

1. What do you like best about our library media program and services?

2. What would you like most to see changed in our library media program and services?

3. What is the most important job the library media specialist does?

4. Additional comments

Figure 19. Library media survey

	Strongly Agree		Uncertain		Strongly Disagree
1. The library media center provides the services I need and want.	1	2	3	4	5
2. The library media program meets the needs of my students.	1	2	3	4	5
3. The library media specialist is helpful and cooperative.	1	2	3	4	5
4. The library media center is an important part of our school.	1	2	3	4	5
5. Library media materials are up-to-date and sufficient to meet the needs of students.	1	2	3	4	5
6. Library media equipment is sufficient to meet my needs.	1	2	3	4	5

Comments: _____

_____

_____

_____

_____

_____

_____

Figure 20. Library media questionnaire

The first part of planning is to set goals and objectives. Desired outcomes must be determined before deciding how to achieve these goals. Goals are the end results; objectives are the means to reach goals. For instance, a goal could be to increase the number of students using the library media center. The objectives selected would focus on ways that goal might be obtained. Objectives might include making the library media center more attractive and inviting and working with teachers to design units incorporating library media activities.

After goals and objectives are selected, all options are examined. Brainstorming can be very effective here and the library media specialist should take advantage of the ideas of the entire library media center staff. Brainstorming involves creatively searching for solutions to the identified concerns. At this point, all ideas, no matter how impractical, are included. Next, the specialist carefully reviews the list and decides which ideas will be most effective in achieving the objective. The options that seem to have the best chance of succeeding are selected.

These options should be critically analyzed for risks and benefits. There are always risks of some kind, but actions should be as risk-free as possible. The library media specialist should also consider hidden risks. The benefits should be critiqued to determine whether they will be sufficient to meet the goal. Other concerns at this point are costs and resources. A fantastic plan will work only if funds are available, people are committed and involved, and material resources can be readily tapped.

At this point the library media specialist has evolved a clear, feasible plan. The next task is to decide who will do what and when it will be done. A time line is designed to inform everyone what has to be accomplished, who is to do it, and when it is to be completed. Sufficient time for minor delays should be built into the time line so that unplanned setbacks do not result in a breakdown of the entire plan.

Accomplishing the plan requires the commitment and support of all those involved. Everyone who will have a part in the public relations activity should be involved in the planning and decision-making process.

Communication

If a good job of planning has been done, the message is ready to be delivered to the audience. Too often this third step is considered as the only one by library media specialists but, without the research and planning steps, the action may not be as successful as desired.

A successful public relations event depends on timing, repetition, and follow-through. Timing means scheduling the event at the most auspicious time possible when there will be minimal disruption or conflict. Repetition means providing sufficient exposure so those individuals to whom the event is directed are sure to be aware of what is happening. When public relations events are ongoing, the public relations value increases dramatically. Not every public relations action needs to be repeated, but follow-through of some kind is essential to ensure continued visibility and interest. A one-time event will result in little long-term change unless there is consistent follow-through.

Evaluation

A public relations event is not finished when the activity takes place. After the event, it is time for the library media specialist to take a long, hard look at what occurred. The planning as well as the implementation should be examined to determine what succeeded and what could have been improved. The specialist should analyze what worked best and why. It is also important to discover any flaws and consider if these could have been predicted. The purpose is to prevent the same problems from arising the next time.

Collecting feedback from the audience provides more data. The library media specialist should select an evaluation tool that is appropriate for the event. Responses from surveys, logs, reader-interest studies, informal interviews, or grapevine feedback can help the library media specialist judge whether the goals and objectives were achieved.

On completion of the evaluation process, one cycle of the four-step process has been enacted. Public relations is considered to be a cycle because completion leads back to the first step where the process begins again with research. Following the four-step public relations process makes public relations activities meaningful and ensures that they are directed to the identified audiences.

Public Relations Techniques

The public relations action described in step three of the public relations process can encompass a wide variety of activities. There are both informal and formal approaches.

Informal Public Relations

Informal public relations techniques are those used every day as the library media specialist communicates with various people in the school setting. Everything said and done by the library media specialist has an affect, however slight, on others in the school community. For this reason, it is important that the library media specialist be aware that every action is viewed by others in either a positive or a negative way.

One of the most subtle ways in which people judge the library media program is by the image projected by the specialist. Most people tend to judge others initially by appearance, dress, manner, and bearing. Clothing should be neat and attractive and should convey a professional look. This is not to say that a plain, navy blue suit is required at all times. The most important aspect of clothing is neatness. Clothes should be in good repair and appropriate for the work being done.

The way an individual stands, walks, and talks also subtly influences others. Acting with self-assurance and confidence while maintaining a friendly manner projects an attitude of competence and professionalism. Small gestures, such as a friendly smile, are important. Courtesies extended to all may have powerful implications.

Secretaries, custodians, volunteers, and substitutes often have contacts that can have far-reaching consequences for the library media program. Everyone should be considered as a potential supporter and advocate.

Formal Public Relations

Formal public relations communications are those that go through a more elaborate planning process and include an end product. These activities may be undertaken by an individual library media specialist attempting to influence a single school community or they may be implemented at the district, state, or national level to increase public awareness of library media programs.

Communiques

Written communications can be a low-key but effective means of public relations. Commercial or locally designed forms using a consistent logo and format will bring the library media center to mind when communications are received by faculty and students. Brochures and bookmarks are frequently used for communicating a specific message. Notices about new materials, materials that have been recommended and are now available, and even requests for the return of materials all have public awareness implications.

Newsletters

Newsletters are an excellent means of communication. They can be very simple and intended to inform teachers and staff of happenings in the library media center. Newsletters can be used to remind teachers of available services, to announce new acquisitions, and to publicize the skills being taught to students. Newsletters to parents are an effective tool. The school may already produce a newsletter that is sent to parents and, if so, the library media specialist should try to include at least one news item about the library media center in every newsletter sent home. A district-level library media newsletter keeps library media specialists informed and can serve as a public relations tool for communication to a larger audience within the district. When sent to administrators, board of education members, and legislators as well as members of the library media community, it keeps others abreast of new developments in the district's library media centers.

A good newsletter should be well written, concise, and free of spelling and typing errors. It is essential to proofread copy and, if at all possible, have someone else check for comprehension and errors. Due to poor copy quality, a ditto machine should not be used to make copies. Unless the print is legible, the intended audience will not take time to read the content. The newsletter need not be long. One page full of interesting, worthwhile news is better than pages of boring, trivial minutia.

Presentations

Short, to-the-point presentations at faculty and PTA meetings can be an effective communication method. Whenever possible, the specialist should use these presentations as an example of effectively using the media technology available in the school. Two to five minutes should be the maximum time for this type of interaction, which can include a variety of topics of interest to the assembled group.

When the library media specialist makes a presentation at a local, state, or national conference, it can enhance the specialist's reputation and hence that of the program. The conference may be for library media coordinators or, better yet, for another group. Reading, curriculum, and other conferences need skilled workshop presenters. Tying library media skills into a related topic is an excellent means of improving the image of the library media program.

Staff In-service Training

In-service training workshops, aimed at helping teachers gain new skills and techniques with media materials, are another good public relations method. In-service training sessions should be voluntary as requiring teachers to attend may create animosity rather than further good public relations. As teachers discover that in-service workshops are useful and meet their perceived needs, they will see the value of attending.

Quarterly and Annual Reports

Reports, regularly given to the school principal, are effective in assessing achievement and services. They are an important public relations tool as research information and evaluation are provided through the principal's perceptions and feedback.

Special Events

Special events require coordination and extensive planning and may be the beginning or culminating activity in a year-long plan. These activities should use the four-step public relations process in detail. Some activities frequently used to communicate the library media mission are read-ins, book fairs, media fairs (designed to acquaint teachers with new acquisitions), open houses, teas, breakfasts, and tours (for new staff members and parents).

School Library Media Month, held nationwide in April, is a good time for many special public relations activities. A variety of promotional materials and publications available from AASL provide ideas for building support for school library media goals.

John Cotton Dana Awards

John Cotton Dana Awards are presented yearly by the H. W. Wilson Company for excellence in public relations programs. JCD Awards are given for well-rounded, year-long programs that are multifaceted in reaching current and potential patrons. Special awards are given for public relations programs aimed at a specific audience during a limited period of time. School library media center entries form one category within the awards system. Entries are judged by how effectively the four-step process was used and how successfully the goals and objectives were met.

The process of entering the contest is beneficial to library media specialists because it requires the specialist to review all aspects of the public relations program. When a school or district wins a John Cotton Dana Award, local and national publicity confer additional benefits.

Summary

Public relations is an ongoing aspect of an effective library media program. The four-step process of research, planning, communication, and evaluation is used to change and strengthen attitudes and concepts held by designated publics. Informal public relations are ongoing behaviors of the knowledgeable library media specialist. Formal public relations require more extensive planning and have, as an end result, an event or activity designed for a specific purpose with a target audience.

CHAPTER 14

Professional Strategies

Developing and implementing operational procedures and techniques, as described in previous chapters of this book, constitute one aspect of the library media specialist's role. This is a demanding position and it is important that the specialist maintain a balanced perspective toward it. This chapter will focus on creating strategies for preventing burnout, finding support networks, and using professional organizations to keep abreast of issues and concerns.

Avoiding Burnout

Library media specialists are susceptible to the malignant malady of burnout because of characteristics inherent in the position. Often the specialist operates in isolation; this is especially true if the specialist functions without other professional and support staff or must serve more than one school. Teachers talk to other teachers who have the same basic concerns and problems, but when no one in the school faces the same struggles as the library media specialist, this support system is absent. Teachers may not even understand why the library media specialist feels stress because they do not fully comprehend the magnitude of the job.

The diversity and constant flexibility required to function effectively in a library media center can be stimulating, but it can also become a source of frustration. Dedicated to helping everyone find and use the materials they need, the specialist may feel inadequate when it is impossible to fulfill all requests. Management functions, such as order deadlines, mail, inventory, or processing new materials, are never ending. The challenge of keeping abreast of rapidly changing technology exerts additional pressures. The specialist is also constantly aware of major tasks that should be done, such as rejuvenating the card catalog, converting to a database, or processing backlogs of uncataloged materials. Even though it is obvious that these tasks cannot be accomplished overnight, they lurk in the subconscious. To adequately handle these conflicting demands, coping skills are needed.

Avoiding burnout should be a priority concern before it becomes a problem. A library media specialist accepts a position in a school with a sense of enormous energy and enthusiasm, making ambitious long-range plans and taking on many projects. Maintaining this positive outlook is a challenge and a necessity if the specialist is to retain peak levels of energy and commitment. The following stress reduction techniques are tried and true and, in many cases, only common sense. It is important that the library media specialist keep these points in mind regardless of whether the job is old or new.

Balance work and play. A fresh outlook and solutions to problems may occur when the specialist finds time for relaxation. A hobby or other outside interest can provide a focus for nonprofessional pursuits. Everyone needs two separate lives—a work life and a home life. Each balances the other. The library media specialist should find some time each day for personal interests. Time for family and friends should be a priority for the library media specialist. Working twelve hours a day does not leave energy for interaction with these important people and a life without balance can develop stress that leads to burnout.

Exercise. Exercise, such as tennis, aerobic dance, brisk walking, or participation in any physical activity a minimum of three times a week, is essential for preventing burnout. Exercise has the added benefit of improving health and energy levels. A person who is exhausted at the end of the workday often feels revitalized after an hour of vigorous exercise.

Positive attitude. A positive attitude can do wonders for avoiding the burnout syndrome. Adopting a Pollyanna approach of always smiling and avoiding anything unpleasant is not constructive, but being optimistic in realistic ways helps keep the focus on the positives of life rather than the negatives. Constant exposure to negative people can slowly erode a positive outlook. While it is not possible to avoid negative people on the job (library media specialists should work with all faculty members regardless of their gloomy nature) developing friendships with people who impart a positive example helps counter that exposure.

Time management. Using time effectively is essential if the library media specialist hopes to avoid getting bogged down in daily routine and trivia. This book has provided techniques for managing some of the time-consuming chores that have the potential of controlling the life of the specialist. Organizing the inventory system and streamlining the circulation process are steps toward effective time management, but these are not the only tasks that assume gigantic proportions if not properly managed. Some housekeeping details can take an inordinate amount of time if they are not organized. A neat desk and orderly filing cabinets facilitate the daily routine as minutes saved in locating information add up to hours. Files should be weeded at least once a year. Outdated catalogs and other materials that once had meaning, but are no longer useful, should be removed.

Delegation, whenever possible, is an effective way of handling many routine tasks. Cards may not be interfiled perfectly into the card catalog when students add them, but it is much faster to correct a few errors before dropping the cards onto the rod than it is to find the correct spot for each of the cards. Living with the fact that every item will not be in its exact location on the shelves at all times eliminates some frustration and saves time. Teaching students to reshelve books and materials carefully and then accepting the fact that perfection is not possible is an effective management technique.

Big jobs often seem overwhelming when looked at as a whole. Breaking each big job down into manageable components and doing a small task each day makes it possible to complete a big project in a reasonable amount of time.

Forms for frequently repeated communications with teachers and students are another time-saver. Forms, such as overdue book and fine reports, can be purchased or they can be handmade to fit the situation.

A library media specialist newly assigned to a school should begin to offer services slowly. It is much easier to expand services and extend additional assistance and options than it is to reduce services after they have been initiated. The extent of services is directly related to the number of staff available. The 1988 standards, *Information Power,* provide guidelines for preferred staffing levels and for matching services to staff responsibilities.

Checklists are valuable when the quantity of work to be done appears monumental. As each item is checked off the list, there is a sense of moving toward completion of specific tasks. Opening and closing of the library media center each year creates additional work that sometimes gets overlooked due to conflicting demands at those busy times of the year. Checklists ensure that nothing important is overlooked. For the new library media specialist, the checklist provides direction. Rather than compiling a random list, it is helpful to prioritize in accordance with established or desired time lines. For example, retrieving audiovisual equipment from classrooms precedes checking and cleaning each item and cleaning precedes sending equipment out for repairs. It is not necessary, however, to spend extensive time prioritizing; many jobs will overlap and others will occur simultaneously.

Goal setting. It is important for library media specialists to have long-term goals. Deciding what is to be accomplished in the next month, the next year, even the next ten years, gives direction and focus to the program. These goals can be as diverse as making changes in the library media center or in the library media program, getting an advanced degree, or aspiring to move to a supervisor's position. Goals need to be set and plans made to reach them. Assessment at regular intervals keeps them in proper focus. Before one goal is actually achieved, it is important that another be at least partially formulated. Goals are not static and unchanging, but should be flexible to allow for a change of direction if interests or situations change.

Continuing education. Most people never reach the point where they know everything they want to know. An active curiosity and thirst for knowledge should be lifelong pursuits. There are always new insights to be gained, procedural shortcuts to learn, and tips for improving the library media center and its program. District staff development programs, especially those designed for library media specialists, can provide valuable information.

Special workshops are another source of continuing education. Workshops may cover topics of general interest or may focus on specific themes. They do not have to be strictly library media oriented to be beneficial.

University courses provide an excellent mode for keeping up-to-date in the library media field. Classes can be audited if credit is not needed or wanted. In areas where the nearest university is too far away to be a feasible option, courses are sometimes offered on educational television. Many of these courses give the same credit as their on-campus counterparts. Correspondence courses are another option.

Community education is an additional avenue of continuing education. Many school districts have extensive offerings in these programs and almost everyone can find a class that will interest them.

Emotional balance. Maintaining a sense of humor and the ability to laugh, no matter how difficult circumstances become, keeps things in perspective. No matter how grim a situation seems, in ten years it probably will have been forgotten, or at least it will not seem so serious. By keeping a balanced perspective, overreacting to situations that may blow over and disappear is avoided. This does not mean that all problems can be laughed away. Rather, by considering all sides of a problem and then stepping back a little, it may be possible to discover innovative and creative solutions that are missed when the atmosphere is too intense.

Networking

Building a support network of colleagues in the library media field is especially important as the specialist attempts to fulfill the requirements of the job. No one is an expert at handling every problem and questions arise that need to be answered. A network of colleagues can be helpful in many ways.

Sharing common concerns. Networking puts the isolated library media specialist into contact with others who share similar circumstances and working concerns. These individuals provide a valuable listening service by just being there when the specialist needs someone to talk to who will understand common frustrations and concerns. A two-way exchange such as this can be very supportive, especially if it is readily available by the simple means of dialing the telephone.

Idea sharing. Networking provides a medium for sharing ideas. No one can be constantly creative and devise novel lesson plans, bulletin boards, and special programs on a regular basis. An idea developed by one person may be revised and adapted by others to fit their own needs. Brainstorming ideas in a group may generate several others.

Work sharing. Work sharing is a relatively old concept, but one not frequently used by library media specialists. This neglected art can be a boon to sanity and accomplishment, especially when available staff is not sufficient for the level of service desired. To successfully share work requires two or three specialists who can work together and who have a similar need, but who do not necessarily have the same strengths and abilities. Another option is to organize a small team from the network (no more than five) and designate a specific project for each.

Work sharing requires some preliminary planning and organization. The work that will be done together should be selected and a time to do it set. Inventory, card catalog updating, and weeding are three tasks that can be done more than twice as fast if two people do them instead of one. When sharing work, it is important that the time spent in each school be equitably allocated and that each person involved be committed to putting in the agreed-upon time. These shared workdays are best when they do not interfere with the regular operation of the library media center, for example, extended days beyond the regular school calendar. It is vital that principals be consulted before making arrangements so that the necessary support is generated and there are no misconceptions.

Resource sharing. Resource sharing is fairly common at the university level, but is only beginning to surface in elementary and secondary schools. However, when budgets are less than adequate, sharing resources may be one answer to providing needed materials.

Sharing materials works best with professional books and audiovisual materials. If library media specialists in two schools subscribe to two different professional periodicals and make arrangements to trade them, each will have access to two review sources for the price of one. If a teacher needs a sound filmstrip for one week of the year, it may be possible to borrow it rather than buy it. Books intended for student use are less adaptable for interschool loan because they need to be readily available within the school. Occasionally, however, this may be a viable option. By building an interschool library loan arrangement within a district, library media specialists increase the resources available.

Building a network is one way for library media specialists to gain support on the job. Developing the necessary contacts is important. In-district networks are usually the easiest to establish as there is opportunity for frequent contact with other library media specialists through district meetings and workshops. Out-of-district networks can be developed through participation in professional organizations or university classes.

Networks may be formal or informal. Informal networks maintain contact through telephone calls, lunches or other random events. Formal networks, on the other hand, provide contacts through planned meetings and organized activities.

Professional Organizations

Becoming a member of a professional organization is part of being a professional. Library media specialists not only need the benefits of professional teaching associations, but also those devoted to the library media profession. This can seem like a financial burden, but there are distinct benefits derived from active membership in these organizations. A variety of interesting people having similar aspirations and problems belong to an association. Contact with specialists from other districts provides the library media specialist with a rich resource pool from which to draw ideas.

The journals and periodicals published by professional groups are instrumental in keeping library media specialists abreast of current research and practice. These journals offer expert advice on a variety of subjects, provide a forum for intellectual concerns, and often furnish answers to problems that have not been solved locally.

Conferences sponsored by professional library media associations provide an opportunity for renewal and growth that cannot be overemphasized. Attending a conference can stimulate enthusiasm and dedication and make work a joyful pursuit.

The diversity of professional organizations is overwhelming and confusing to the new library media specialist. It is recommended that library media specialists become members of local, state, and national organizations to benefit from the support of each, but that active participation begin at the local level and, as the specialist becomes more involved, expand to state and national levels.

Local or regional associations. Local or regional organizations provide the greatest opportunity for the new library media specialist to become involved. The concerns addressed by these associations are usually those of greatest interest to the representative group. Opportunities abound for serving on committees and taking leadership roles. Contacts made with other members of the group can be beneficial to the library media specialist who is building a network of support.

State organizations. State organizations are another excellent professional connection. Participation at the state level brings association with library media counterparts from across an entire state. State organizations usually have well-planned conferences that provide an excellent method of keeping in touch with new technology, techniques, and materials. As travel to distant parts of the country is not involved, participation is usually fairly inexpensive.

National associations. National associations provide a line of communication that spans the country and furnishes a national viewpoint. The American Library Association and its division the American Association of School Librarians connect the local library media specialist to the global concerns of the profession. Within AASL, the Affiliate Assembly provides a direct link from state organizations to the national association. ALA has a yearly summer conference that offers a multitude of programs addressing diverse needs and concerns. A midwinter conference is devoted to committee work. AASL holds a fall conference every two or three years that examines issues of interest to the school library media specialist.

ALA, AASL and other divisions within ALA actively encourage members to participate on committees. By doing so, members have direct involvement in shaping the profession.

The Association for Educational Communications and Technology (AECT) is a national organization that concentrates on technology and media concerns. Yearly spring conferences provide members with a look at the cutting edge of technology with ideas for implementing the technology into school programs. A library media specialist who is considering implementation of technological innovations will find information readily available.

ALA, AASL, and AECT all publish professional journals that keep members apprised of current research and trends. These periodicals are a tangible aspect of membership in the organization. Intangible reasons for membership include being a part of a large network of individuals sharing common problems and ideas and feeling connected to the pulse of the profession.

Regardless of the level of involvement, the library media specialist finds that belonging to a professional organization increases professional outlook and growth. Benefits far exceed financial investment when the library media specialist becomes involved as an active participating member in such groups.

Summary

Burnout is not inevitable. Avoiding it takes conscious thought and effort on the part of the library media specialist, but it is too important an issue to be ignored. There are many excellent books available that deal specifically with this topic. To keep a healthy attitude, the library media specialist should balance work and play, exercise regularly, be positive, manage time effectively, have goals, continue learning, and retain a sense of humor. Formal and informal networks with others having similar concerns are beneficial in generating shared ideas, work, and resources. Active membership in a professional organization expands contact with other professionals and provides a forum for the dissemination of ideas and research.

Notes

Chapter 1

1. C. C. Certain, "The Elementary-School Library Defined in Terms of Book Conservation and Library Service," *Elementary School Journal* 24 (January 1924): 360.

2. Mary Peacock Douglas, "Functions and Standards for a School Library," *School Executive* 64 (December 1944): 50.

3. Eleanor Ahlers, "How Will the New School Library Standards Affect High School Libraries," *High School Journal* 43 (November 1959): 42–45.

4. "School Libraries Get $1 Million Plus From Knapp Foundation," *Wilson Library Bulletin* 37 (December 1962): 317.

5. Ibid.

6. James Robert Yarling, "Children's Understandings and Use of Selected Library-Related Skills in Two Elementary Schools, One With and One Without a Centralized Library," (Ed.D. dissertation, Ball State University, 1968).

7. David Dempsey, "The Best Title of All," *Saturday Review* 49 (October 1, 1966): 50.

8. Lillian N. Gerhardt, "Talking About ESEA," *School Library Journal* 32, no. 4 (December 1985): 2.

9. Ibid.

10. James C. Baughman, "The Meaning of the Standards for School Library Media Programs," *School Media Quarterly* 1 (Summer 1973): 275.

11. Christopher Wright, "Washington News," *School Media Quarterly* 3 (Fall 1974): 76–77.

12. *Media Programs: District and School* (Chicago: ALA, 1975 and Washington, D.C.: AECT, 1975), vii.

13. Elizabeth B. Mann, "Federal Government, 1983," in *School Library Media Annual 1984*, ed. Shirley L. Aaron and Pat R. Scales, vol. 2 (Littleton, Colo.: Libraries Unlimited, 1984), 55.

14. *School Library Media Annual 1987*, ed. Shirley L. Aaron and Pat R. Scales, vol. 5 (Littleton, Colo.: Libraries Unlimited, 1987), 49.

15. *Legislative Report of the ALA Washington Office, Jan.–June:* 1989: 4, and Appendix A.

16. Eileen D. Cooke, "Issues Alert," *School Library Media Quarterly* 16 (Fall 1988) : 48.

17. E. Blanche Woolls and David V. Loertscher, *The Microcomputer Facility and the School Library Media Specialist* (Chicago: ALA, 1986), 2.

18. Ibid., 2–3.

19. *Media Programs: District and School*, 34–35.

20. John T. Gillespie, *A Model School District Media Program: Montgomery County as a Case Study* (Chicago: ALA, 1977), 16–17.

21. Ron Blazek, *Influencing Students toward Media Center Use: An Experimental Investigation in Mathematics* (Chicago: ALA, 1975), 119.

22. David Loertscher, "The Second Revolution: A Taxonomy for the 1980s," *Wilson Library Bulletin* 56, no. 6 (Fall 1982): 417–421.

23. *Information Power: Guidelines for School Library Media Programs* (Chicago: ALA, 1988), p. 21.

24. Ibid., 35.

25. Margaret E. Chisholm and Donald P. Ely, *Instructional Design and the Library Media Specialist* (Chicago: ALA, 1979), 7.

26. Barbara Stripling, "What Price ID? A Practical Approach to a Personal Dilemma," *School Library Media Quarterly* 12, no. 4. (Summer 1984):290.

Chapter 3

1. Warren B. Hicks, " Managing the Building Level School Library Media Program," in *School Media Centers: Focus on Trends and Issues,* no. 7 (Chicago: ALA, 1981): 7–8.

2. David Loertscher, "The Second Revolution: A Taxonomy for the 1980s," *Wilson Library Bulletin* 56, no. 6 (Fall 1982):417–421.

3. *Information Power: Guidelines for School Library Media Programs* (Chicago: ALA, 1988), 117–139.

Chapter 4

1. *Information Power: Guidelines for School Library Media Programs* (Chicago: ALA, 1988), 122.

2. Dale W. Brown and Nancy A. Newman, "Regional Networking and Collection Management in School Library Media Centers," in *Collection Management for School Library Media Centers,* ed. Brenda White (New York: the Haworth Press, 1986), 151.

3. David V. Loertscher, "Administrative Uses," in *The Microcomputer Facility and the School Library Media Specialist* (Chicago: ALA, 1986), 61–64.

4. Ibid., 62–64.

5. Elizabeth Hoffman, "Ten Commandments for Media Center Planners," in *Media Center Facilities Design* (Chicago: ALA, 1978), 33.

Chapter 5

1. Ron Blazek, *Influencing Students toward Media Center Use: An Experimental Investigation in Mathematics* (Chicago: ALA, 1975), 141.

2. Ibid., 132.

3. *Information Power: Guidelines for School Library Media Programs* (Chicago: ALA, 1988), 132–138.

4. Ibid., 28

Chapter 6

1. Robert N. Broadus, *Selecting Materials for Libraries,* 2d ed., (New York: H. W. Wilson, 1981), 11.

2. *Intellectual Freedom Manual,* 3d ed. (Chicago: ALA, 1989), 171.

3. Ruth Ann Davies, *The School Library Media Center: A Force For Educational Excellence,* 2d ed., (New York: R. R. Bowker Co., 1974), 87.

4. Dorothy M. Broderick, *Library Work with Children* (New York: H. W. Wilson Co., 1977), 4.

5. Ibid., 7.

6. David V. Loertscher, "Collection Mapping: An Evaluation Strategy for Collection Development," *Drexel Library Quarterly* 21, no. 2 (Spring 1985): 11–12.

7. Ibid., 10–11.

8. Ibid., 16–17.

9. William Murray et al., "Collection Mapping and Collection Development," *Drexel Library Quarterly* 21, no. 2 (Spring 1985), 40–46.

10. Patsy H. Perritt, "Censorship in School Libraries: Problems and Strategies," in *School Library Media Annual 1984, Volume Two* (Littleton, Colo.: Libraries Unlimited, 1984), 24.

Chapter 7

1. Lillian N. Gerhardt, "Half-a-Book Onward," *School Library Journal* 33, no. 3 (November 1986): 4.

2. "Action Exchange," *American Libraries* 17, no. 1 (January 1986): 14.

Chapter 8

1. Robert E. Chase and Jane Klasing, "Creating Management Software," *The Microcomputer and the School Library Media Specialist* (Chicago: ALA, 1986), 79.

Chapter 9

1. Betty Costa and Marie Costa, *A Micro Handbook for Small Libraries and Media Centers* (Littleton, Colo.: Libraries Unlimited, 1983), 77.

Chapter 11

1. Carol Tenopir, "Online Searching in Schools," *Library Journal* 111, no. 2 (February 1, 1986): 60–61.

Chapter 12

1. "Personnel," in *Information Power: Guidelines for School Library Media Programs* (Chicago: ALA, 1988), 65.

Bibliography

Achieving Accountability; Readings on the Evaluation of Media Centers. Chicago: ALA, 1981.

Blazek, Ron. *Influencing Students toward Media Center Use.* Chicago: ALA, 1975.

Censorship Litigation and the Schools; Proceedings of a Colloquium Held January 1981. Chicago: ALA, 1983.

Costa, Betty, and Marie Costa. *A Micro Handbook for Small Libraries and Media Centers.* Littleton, Colo.: Libraries Unlimited, 1986.

Edsall, Marian S. *Practical PR for School Library Media Centers.* New York: Neal-Schuman Publishers, 1984.

Gillespie, John T. *A Model School District Media Program,* ALA Studies in Librarianship, no. 6. Chicago: ALA, 1977.

Information Power: Guidelines for School Library Media Programs. Chicago: ALA, 1988.

Intellectual Freedom Manual. 2d ed. Chicago: ALA, 1983.

Jones, Frances M. *Defusing Censorship.* Phoenix, Ariz.: Oryx Press, 1983.

Kids and Libraries. Seattle, Wash.: Dyad Services, 1984.

Kies, Cosette. *Projecting a Positive Image Through Public Relations.* School Media Centers: Focus on Trends and Issues, no. 2. Chicago: ALA, 1978.

Kohn, Rita, and Krysta Tepper. *Have You Got What They Want? P.R.'s Strategies for the School Librarian/Media Specialist: A Workbook.* Metuchen, N.J.: Scarecrow Press, 1982.

Kulleseid, Eleanor R. *Beyond Survival to Power for School Library Media Professionals.* Hamden, Conn.: Shoe String Press, 1985.

Libraries and the Learning Society; Papers in Response to "A Nation at Risk." Chicago: ALA, 1984.

Martin, Betty. *A Survival Handbook for the School Library Media Specialist.* Hamden, Conn.: Shoe String Press, 1983.

Martin, Betty, and Ben Carson. *The Principal's Handbook on the School Library Media Center.* Syracuse, N.Y.: Gaylord Professional Publications, 1978.

Miller, Inabeth. *Microcomputers in School Library Media Centers.* New York: Neal-Schuman Publishers, 1984.

Naumer, Janet Noll. *Media Center Management with an Apple II.* Littleton, Colo.: Libraries Unlimited, 1984.

Prostano, Emanuel T., and Joyce S. Prostano. *Case Studies in Library/Media Management.* Littleton, Colo.: Libraries Unlimited, 1982.

————*The School Library Media Center.* Library Science Text Series. Littleton, Colo.: Libraries Unlimited, 1977.

School Librarianship. Elmsford, N.Y.: Pergamon Press, 1981.

Taggart, Dorothy T. *Management and Administration of the School Library Media Program.* Hamden, Conn.: Library Professional Publications, 1980.

Thomason, Nevada Wallis. *Circulation Systems for School Library Media Centers.* Littleton, Colo.: Libraries Unlimited, 1985.

Toor, Ruth, and Hilda K. Weisburg. *The Complete Book of Forms for Managing the School Library.* West Nyack, N.Y.: The Center for Applied Research in Education, 1982.

Troutner, Joanne. *The Media Specialist, the Microcomputer and the Curriculum*. Littleton, Colo.: Libraries Unlimited, 1983.

Turner, Philip M. *Handbook for School Media Personnel*. Littleton, Colo.: Libraries Unlimited, 1980.

Van Orden, Phyllis. *The Collection Program in Elementary and Middle Schools*. Littleton, Colo.: Libraries Unlimited, 1982.

White, Brenda. *Collection Management for School Library Media Centers*. New York: Haworth Press, 1986.

Woolls, E. Blanche, and David V. Loertscher. *The Microcomputer Facility and the School Library Media Specialist*. Chicago: ALA, 1986.

Index

Prepared by Pamela Hori